Making

Hats

MAKING
Hats

ALISON HART

THE CROWOOD PRESS

First published in 2019 by
The Crowood Press Ltd
Ramsbury, Marlborough
Wiltshire SN8 2HR

www.crowood.com

British Library Cataloguing-in-Publication Data
A catalogue record for this book is available from the British Library.

ISBN 978 1 78500 493 3

Frontispiece
A shaped bridal headpiece covered with silk and Chantilly lace. The hat is trimmed with a vintage-style silver and pearl brooch and has a semicircular veil that covers the forehead.

Dedication
This book is dedicated to my family and my invaluable feline helpers. Firstly, my ever-supportive and understanding husband Gary who puts up with all my creative mess; to Snarf – my expert finder of stray feathers and chaser of unattended thimbles; to Tilly – to whom veiling is simply irresistible whether attached to a hat or not; and especially to all my family for always believing in me and all my mad ideas.

Acknowledgements
I would like to thank a few people for their help and support in the process of writing this book. First, my husband Gary and my family for all their invaluable support, guidance and advice.

   All the teachers who have shared their millinery knowledge with me, without whom I would not know any of these techniques. The teams of dedicated hat fans at the various millinery suppliers around the country who provide such high-quality materials and super-speedy mail order delivery, in particular Michelle and Fiona at Petershams, Baxter Hart and Abraham and Hat Blocks Direct.

   The Shaws, Michaela Clegg and Lynn Kimber for loaning their completed hats back to me for the final photo shoot.

   Pete Sellwood, Rhiannon Evans, Chris Moles, Gillian Boyd and all my colleagues within the BA Costume and Performance Design and BA Make-Up for Media and Performance courses at AUB.

   Finally, a huge thank you to Snarf and Tilly my ever-helpful assistants.

Typeset by Jean Cussons Typesetting, Diss, Norfolk
Printed and bound in India by Replika Press Pvt Ltd

CONTENTS

INTRODUCTION AND INFORMATION

Introduction

The purpose of this book is for you to learn how to make unique hats and headpieces to wear for special occasions or for every day, and also for the fun of creating pretty and wearable accessories. It is designed to inspire and enable the making of hats for everyday wear following traditional construction methods using both specialist millinery materials and a range of fabrics and trimmings.

A hat does not need to have any one specific shape – hats can be different sizes, colours and styles; with a brim or without. There is a shape to suit every head, hairstyle and hat-wearing occasion. They are limited only by the imagination of the maker and wearer. A special outfit is completed and enhanced by a fantastic hat, but everyday hats can be just as eye-catching by using bright colours, pretty trims and exquisite shapes – perhaps just with fewer feathers!

Each of the chapters in this book will introduce new ideas, different materials and fresh techniques to work through that show how the careful choice of each component can accentuate the hat. Each hat is a stand-alone project and the book begins with hats that are simple or fast to make. As you progress through the chapters, the required skills and techniques

LEFT: **A fawn-coloured felt hat, blocked over an oval base and trimmed with fabric flowers that cover three-quarters of the surface of the hat.**

diversify, building to Chapter 8 where the hats are more complex, have couture overtones and require more time and skill to complete.

You may have a particular occasion that requires a hat, or perhaps you just want the challenge of making something new. Whatever your reasons for reading this book, it goes without saying that exciting millinery draws attention and compliments, and makes everyone stand out in a crowd. So this book will help you to complete your own millinery projects to wear however you choose.

My own passion for hats began with wearing them regularly as a teenager. I had several hats that I wore all the time, matching them to my everyday outfits, and I loved wearing them. I was hooked on hats and, having always been creative, began to wonder about making my own. I was offered the opportunity to learn how to make couture hats by attending a course in London. That course was at the London College of Fashion and was run by the late Andrew Bristow. Under his careful guidance and abundant enthusiasm my passion for making hats flourished. I realized that with some instruction I could learn to make hats properly, using the correct millinery techniques. This appealed to my fashion and textiles background, so I attended many subsequent courses. I also completed NCFE (Northern Council for Further Education) qualifications in millinery, during which I met another inspirational millinery tutor, Hillary Peach, who was instrumental in furthering my millinery education.

A midnight navy felt hat worn at an angle with a tapered crown and a luxurious scattering of rose-gold Jaipur lace flowers and foliage.

I continue to attend courses and use millinery books – old and new – to learn new and refine current techniques whilst experimenting with materials to discover new ones. I enjoy making and experimenting as you can never stop learning new creative techniques.

A Brief History of Millinery

'People don't wear hats anymore' is a statement that is often said; but, happily for those of us who love hats, it is no longer true. The twenty-first century has seen a resurgence in interest for wearing hats through celebrities in the public eye wearing more hats, hats being seen in films and new trends in high street fashion. Music stars such as Paloma Faith, Pharrell, Boy George, Lady Gaga, Taylor Swift and Bruno Mars all regularly wear hats in their performances and TV appearances; this kind of exposure helps to make hats more desirable and acceptable. Other stars who famously and regularly wear hats include Sarah Jessica Parker, Christina Aguilera, Johnny Depp, Justin Timberlake, Jennifer Lopez, Samuel L. Jackson, Noel Fielding, Elton John and Olly Murs.

Throughout history hats and headwear have been important for many reasons. We use hats differently today – and their use continues to evolve – but hats still make us feel special and have the ability to change how we feel.

The history of the hat and hat-wearing goes back to the earliest dress records with early hats being more like head coverings, for example veils used for religious or ceremonial purposes. Whilst this has not changed, the hat has also emerged in different areas of our lives. Throughout the centuries millinery has evolved and changed. It used to be social convention for people of all classes to keep their heads covered all the time and to not be seen without a hat or head covering of some kind. It was socially unacceptable not to wear a hat and an outfit was not considered complete until a hat was added. Women would have day hats, which were casual caps or bonnets, and evening-wear hats that were much more elaborate and made to match the outfits worn to social events or gatherings. There were even caps that were worn when sleeping.

Even during the twentieth century the attitude to hats has varied through the decades, with styles changing radically from the 1900s to the 1990s. Women's fashions changed faster and more regularly than men's throughout the twentieth century; the same can be said for millinery styles. In the 1900s ladies' hats were wide-brimmed to complement the S-shape silhouette of the fashionable figure. Hats were flamboyantly decorated, and the more feathers a hat sported, the higher the social status of the wearer. The fashionable head-wear for men in the 1900s were top hats for formal occasions and straw boaters, bowlers and fedoras at all other times. With the onset of the First World War, ladies' hat brims became more practical in size and the men wore more military caps.

By the 1920s styles were relaxing after the war. The most restrictive of corsets were going out of fashion and the masses were cutting their hair and wearing close-fitting hats such as the cloche and turban. Men's top hats were shorter and less formal, with homburgs and panamas becoming popular. Flat caps and bowlers were styles that were still worn in most situations.

In the 1930s the cloche remained a favourite style, but ladies' hats began to reduce in size and to perch on the head at an angle. Hats had asymmetric brims and were trimmed with elegant bows. Brimless toques and Tyrolean-style felt hats – brimmed hats with a crown that tapered to a point – were popular too. The trilby was introduced for men, with the bowler being ever popular and the cap also continuing to be a staple headwear style.

During the 1940s war years, ladies wore military caps and, increasingly, practical head-scarves. Hats were not rationed like other items of clothing; however, they remained small in size and perched on the side of the head. The pillbox style became popular and was worn on the top, side or back of the head. Men's hats were mostly military caps, but homburgs, fedo-ras and the pork pie hat were also popular.

The 1950s brought Dior's New Look and hat brims began to broaden to complement this new style. Brims were either straight and shallow or angled down over the eyes. Trims were simple bows and flowers. In the 1960s the

beret, always a popular shape, became famous for being teamed with the Mary Quant mini-skirt, whilst headscarves and androgynous caps remained popular styles. Simple wide-brimmed felt hats were worn, along with the craze for pillboxes following the trend-setting of Jackie Onassis and Audrey Hepburn. More elaborate hairstyles began to overtake hats in popularity and hat-wearing began to decrease.

By the 1970s the trend for wearing the hair long and flowing for both men and women decreased the wearing of hats, except for simple oversized hats with large floppy brims. In the 1980s hats were simply seen as attire for formal occasions, though celebrities such as

Two bright blocked felt hats. The blue hat has a hand-manipulated brim and a royal blue petersham trim. The orange mini trilby is blocked over separate crown and brim blocks before being trimmed with contrasting navy petersham.

Diana, Princess of Wales regularly wore beautiful hats. A keep-fit craze swept far and wide and leisure clothing was the style, so sweatbands and baseball caps were the most popular forms of headwear.

The 1990s saw a resurgence of high-profile millinery on the catwalks of the world with couture designers featuring sculptural and outrageous headwear. For the general public, though, hats remained attire for formal occasions or a practical way to combat the weather. The twenty-first century has, however, so far seen a revival in the wearing of beautiful hats, both for formal occasion wear and more everyday styles.

In the past hats were worn more frequently and were a socially accepted staple of any outfit. Classic examples of outstanding millinery for us to look back on include the many different styles worn by Audrey Hepburn in her films; the simple bowler hat, made even more famous and iconic through the films of Charlie Chaplin; the different colours and sizes of pillbox hat worn by Jackie Onassis, making it the hat to wear for the chic and beautiful; and the hats worn by Winston Churchill and Frank Sinatra, and while these men were very different characters, they both influenced trends that epitomize their respective eras. They all continue to influence trends today.

Another set of famous hat-wearers is Queen Elizabeth II and the British Royal Family. The Queen has worn hats in all colours throughout her reign, and she has found a style – with a small brim and a crown with some height allowing for different kinds of trims – that really suits her. Rachel Trevor-Morgan is one of the most recent milliners to have made hats for the Queen and has now made more than eighty for her. Camilla, Duchess of Cornwall, and Sophie, Countess of Wessex, have worn some elaborate and sculptural hats on formal occasions.

The younger Royals such as Zara Phillips and the Princesses Beatrice and Eugenie often wear beautiful and elaborate designer hats to social gatherings. They also advocate more subdued and subtle styles that are exquisitely made and can be worn more casually. However, it is Catherine, Duchess of Cambridge who has taken hat-wearing to a whole new level of sophistication, favouring hats and headpieces made by the crème de la crème of both young and established millinery designers. With her image and sense of style being photographed so regularly, she is definitely putting millinery firmly back on the accessories must-have list all around the world. Kate has made the perching saucer hat and the modern pillbox her go-to shapes. These are both stylish and chic whilst being practical and wearable.

Ascot Races is famously and traditionally the annual showcase for the most elaborate and elegant hats, with Ladies' Day being a special opportunity for fans of millinery to both wear and see wonderful examples. Some hats are outrageous and headline-grabbing, whilst many are simply beautiful examples of this elegant art.

Now, at the beginning of the twenty-first century, hats are used for two main purposes: the practicalities of warmth and comfort where we wrap up against cold, wet or sunny weather; and to mark special occasions. We will wear a special hat to a party or a wedding, and these can be as elaborate, colourful and fussy as the occasion demands.

Hats are an essential accessory – probably the best accessory for the way in which they can transform an outfit and make the wearer feel special for a special occasion. They enable us to feel dressed up, looking our best and the centre of attention. However, hats are such a versatile part of an outfit or a look that they should be considered for more everyday wear too. There are so many styles and shapes, materials and trimmings, that modern millinery really has no limits.

The Anatomy of a Hat

A hat can be split into different sections with each section having its own name. Regardless of the construction method or material that the hat is made from, the names for these sections are the same. The main parts of a hat are usually the crown and the brim. All hats have a crown and some have a brim too. A brim is not required on all hats; it depends on the style of the hat.

Fitting a Hat to the Head

Hats sit on the head over the hair and this can affect the style and the fit of the hat. The style of the hair must therefore be considered before deciding on a style of hat for the occasion and measuring the head. Modern hairstyles can be complicated and bulky and some hat styles will not fit on or over them. For everyday hats the hair may be tied up or in a ponytail, and this

will also affect how the hat sits on the head. For special occasions the wearer may have their hair in a totally different style to usual, so it is important that the hat is comfortable to wear and fits in with the hairstyle to avoid the wearer feeling that they need to take the hat off. The main aim is to ensure that the wearer is comfortable and feels happy whilst wearing the hat.

Some hats are smaller than the head and will not fit around the entire head. These are described as perching hats and can be attached with a variety of methods. Choosing the right way to attach the hat is important, as it needs to be secure but without the hairband being too tight or the teeth of the comb digging into the head or pulling on the hair, for example. If the hat is to fit around the circumference of the head – for example, a cap – the head will need to be measured.

The most important aspect of making millinery is the head fitting. This should be considered at every stage of hat making, but especially at the beginning and the end of the process. Every hat begins with the head of the model

Crown. The crown is the part of the hat that the head sits inside and is made up of two parts: the tip and the sideband.

Brim. This can be a continuous part of the crown or a separate piece that is stitched to the crown. The brim has a right side and an underside, but some brims are angled or turned up, so sometimes both sides show on the finished hat.

Under Brim. This is the inside of the brim and is usually a feature when the brim is constructed of two layers of fabric.

Tip. The tip is the uppermost part of the crown. Hats can be constructed with this as a separate piece from the sideband. The tip is usually oval in shape and can be flat or curved.

Sideband. The sideband is the side part of the hat that forms the sides of the crown and encircles the head. When the hat is constructed using a flat pattern method, it is joined with a seam at centre back.

Stand. This forms part of the brim when the brim and crown are split into two separate pieces. It allows the brim and crown to be sewn back together once they have both been blocked.

When blocking hoods in two pieces, the whole hood is blocked over the crown block.

The sideband and tip are sewn back together once they are both blocked. The crown goes over the stand and these two pieces are sewn together to complete the hat.

or recipient being carefully measured. This will ensure that the finished hat will fit comfortably and sit correctly on the head. The circumference of the head should be measured just above the eyebrows at the front with the tape measure then going around the fullest part of the head. If the head measurement is taken too low, the hat will not fit over the fullest part of the head.

Another important aspect to consider at this stage is how and when the hat is to be worn. If there is going to be a bulky hairstyle or hairpiece worn under the hat, this may dramatically change the head fitting measurement. Even a small amount of gathered hair can change the head measurement, so take care to always measure the head exactly at the point where the hat will be sitting on the head. For example, just adding 0.5cm to the circumference of the head fitting will alter the measurement by 2cm.

How to Measure Head Sizes

All of these measurements are essential to ensuring that different styles of hats fit and sit on the head in the correct place.

Measure the head around the whole head just above the eyebrows. Keep the tape measure at the same level around the head. To allow the hat to fit correctly, add a bit extra to the measurement by putting a couple of fingers between the head and the tape measure to create some ease. This will also make allowances for the thickness of the material to be used, which can alter the size of the hat. This is the head fitting measurement.

The second measurement to take is over the head from ear to ear.

Finally, measure from the hairline above the forehead, back over the head to the nape of the neck.

INSPIRATION AND DESIGN

Inspiration Sources

Hats can have themes and whole designer collections have been created with a single theme linking each design together. Alternatively, the starting point for a hat might be a particular shape that you know suits you, a need for a comfortable, practical hat to wear, or a special occasion that needs some more individual design thought.

The inspiration for hats can come from any source and can create very different hat designs. There may be a clear source of inspiration: the design could be inspired by a fabric, a trim or the desire to showcase a special show-stopper feather. The end use for the hat can also advise the choices of materials, colour and trims; a hat that is to be worn to a wedding may be made to match an existing outfit, so the colour could already be decided. However, there are other points to consider when designing any hat.

Fabrics and Materials

The material that the hat is made from is an important factor. There are many different materials used in millinery to create the base of the hat. A hat can be blocked in the final fabric or it can be constructed and then covered with a top fabric. Felt, straw and sinamay can be used not only to provide the structure of the hat but also the final finish. These materials are available in different finishes and many different colours.

Felt comes in an almost endless range of colours and provides a solid colour base that can be subtle pastel shades or fiery bright colours. Sinamay can be blocked into large but light shapes that are easy to wear and hold their shape. Sinamay is semi-transparent and different colours of sinamay can be layered up to match a dress fabric. This is an especially useful technique for matching a fabric where two colours are woven together, such as a shot silk. For almost any other kind of fabric, a buckram or Paris net base can be used flat to construct a hat from flat pieces, or blocked over a hat block to create the shape and then covered with the fabric.

Fabrics and millinery materials can be inspirational when designing and making hats. A trim may be the inspiration for a whole hat. There are some unusual and dramatic feathers and flowers available and these can add to or finish a hat perfectly.

Historical Themes

History is always a great source of inspiration for new hats. The shapes, styles, colours and

LEFT: **Art Deco-inspired blocked felt hat with diamante and feather trims.**

fabrics from historical eras can either be echoed or used as an inspiration for a whole new style of headwear. The black felt hat in the photograph is inspired by the styles of Art Deco in the 1920s and 1930s. The shape is a blocked oval hat designed to perch right at the front of the head. The surface of the felt has a pleat in it to give a ridge that runs the entire length of the hat; this is to reflect the draped fabric turbans that were also very popular at this time. The hat has a black arrowhead quill for drama and black coque feathers that add movement and fun to the hat. The popular dances of the time would have made these feathers bob in time to the jazz music. The hat is finished with a fan of feather pieces in greens and yellows and a diamante and button trim. The fan shape was used regularly in Art Deco styles and is synonymous with the era.

Using historical inspiration for modern hats gives the opportunity to observe a different era and to look into the themes and trends of the time.

Practicalities

Hats are also worn for practical reasons such as keeping warm in the cold winter months. The inspiration for hats such as these can be fabrics such as velvets, wools, tweeds or the softest, warmest fleece fabrics. Some modern fleece fabrics are soft and have a flat, even surface, while others are textured and similar to teddy bear fur. This fabric can be incredibly warm and is surprisingly easy to work with. *See* Chapter 6 for berets made with velvet and fleece fabrics.

Practical hats are those that are often the favourite and comfortable shapes that can be worn every day, such the berets and the other flat pattern hats in Chapter 6. These are easy to wear and as well as keeping the head warm and protecting the hair from the weather, they are stylish and comfortable. Another practicality of berets is that they can be rolled up and shoved into a bag without having to worry about storing the hat safely. They will not lose their shape and are ready to wear again as soon as you take them out.

Time

We all lead busy lives where time is of the essence. Luckily there are trims, accessories and hat 'ingredients' available to buy that can create almost instant and diverse headwear. This is a great resource and the components are perfect to work with when time is short. Chapters 4 and 5 have examples of how these ingredients can be used in different ways to create headpieces that are easy to make and unique. The first hat in Chapter 4 uses a simple striped ribbon as the main decoration, which is offset by a feather bundle. The third hat in Chapter 4 has a purple silk flower with a spray of purple veiling. The ingredients are fairly simple, but the finished hat looks sophisticated.

Hats for Occasions

The length of time that a hat will be worn needs to be considered when assessing comfort and practicality for the wearer; a heavy hat will not be tolerated for long, and an uncomfortable wedding hat will be discarded after the ceremony. Smaller lightweight hats tend to be more practical to wear and can still create impact.

Special occasions are a great time to wear something out of the ordinary: a wide-brimmed hat or an explosion of feathers that create movement and drama with every step taken; a splash of colour; or a sophisticated shape.

A collection of basic but useful items including pins, thread, a tape measure, a polystyrene head and hat bases.

Recording Ideas

It is important to record all of your ideas. You may look back on an older idea and be inspired in the future. The design journey can start anywhere and has lots of different avenues to explore.

You can create a mood board to gather many different ideas together and include different colours, textures and even fabric swatches. A mood board can be (but doesn't have to be) an excuse to break out the scissors, glue and scrapbooking skills. However, if this fills you with dread, there are many easy-to-use online versions of pinboards where you can collect your ideas in one place. You can even have a series of pinboards for different hat ideas.

A mood board is a great place to be inspired and to refine your thoughts and ideas. Sometimes this collecting of ideas can really help with the design process. You may end up with more than one idea from this exercise.

Another useful way to collect ideas is to keep a sketchbook or notebook. Inspiration can strike at any time so ensure you can record the details as you find them. Quick sketches and even individual words can jog your memory and remind you of an idea you had. The drawing does not have to be perfect or even finished; it is the idea that matters. Linking words together and seeing where they take you is another option.

Try looking at the colours people team together with outfits, the texture of tree bark, the structure of a flower or how a plant grows new leaves – could you recreate that with fabric and stitches? This can be recorded digitally on phones or tablets, or with more traditional paper notebooks.

Design Considerations

Some shapes of hat suit or do not suit certain face shapes, so this needs to be taken into account. Some faces suit smaller hats that perch on the side of the head and some are better suited to hats with brims large or small. There is a hat shape to complement each face shape and it is especially important that all hats are fitted to the head and sit in the correct place.

Elsa Schiaparelli, who designed and made iconic hats and clothing ranges in the 1930s and 1940s, is quoted as saying: 'one can add pads and bows, one can lower or raise the lines, modify the curves, accentuate this or that point, but the harmony must remain.'

Everyone has a style and shape of hat that suits them. The key is to find that shape. Each

Navy knotted ramie straw sun hat with a stitched headband.

The hat should be easy for the wearer to situate on the head without the maker being there to place it. It should be comfortable to wear, with the time that it will be worn taken into account, and it must stay in place without falling off or unduly getting in the way. For example, if a wedding guest wants to wear their hat all through the ceremony and the wedding meal, they should be able to do this and still be able to eat. The hat should be comfortable to wear so it is almost forgotten about – it is only the compliments the wearer receives that should remind them they are wearing such a fantastic hat!

The design of the hat or headpiece should mostly be a result of the discussions with the person who will wear it.

Balance and Symmetry

Balance is the most important area to get right with hat design. The hat size, shape, colour, materials and trims need to be appropriate for the occasion, and more importantly, the hat should suit the person who will wear it. In millinery boutiques in the height of hat-wearing eras, hats were always made especially for and fitted to each customer individually.

Here are a few guidelines I have learned to follow for designing a successful hat:

- Look for balance and symmetry in the trimmings; when using feathers or flowers, a rule of 1–3–5 works well. A single feather by itself can look very sophisticated and can be a real design feature. Otherwise, always have bunches of flowers or feathers in odd numbers. Three flowers will sit back to back very neatly nestled together and will have the added bonus of hiding any stitches or stems with their petals.
- Feathers also look very effective in bundles.

hat or headpiece is unique and the details of size, colour and trim is decided by the milliner and the wearer. As the maker or wearer of the hat may have a clear idea of what the finished hat is to look like, the key is ensuring that it suits the wearer and the occasion.

Inspiration can come from anywhere: a historical shape may be inspiring; a fabric may lend itself to a particular shape or design; you may want to show a pattern or a colour; sometimes a hat will match, complement or contrast with an outfit. But a golden rule to follow is that the hat must always flatter and complement the wearer.

These can be held together at the base out of sight or added into the design one by one. Feathers are either left-handed or right-handed, and have a natural curve to them depending on which side of the bird they came from. Keep this in mind when creating a bundle of feathers and use their natural curve to enhance the design. Some styles of feathers, such as coque feathers and goose biots, can be curled; this also adds another design feature to the feather.

- Feathers can add height and graceful movement to a hat without adding bulk to the design. Some feathers, such as coque feathers, bob as the wearer walks and can accentuate a beautiful hat. Fixed feathers can also add impact without adding movement. Some people do not like feathers of any kind and will specifically request none at all.
- Try not to overload the design with too many trims. It is possible to have too many flowers or feathers on one hat, making the hat seem too heavy.
- Millinery of all sizes, styles and materials can be made in a rainbow of colours from monochrome to pastel shades, brights to metallics; but choose carefully so that the colours work for the hat and are not overpowering. Contrasts of colour can work as well as those that match tonally.

A cerise pink oval sinamay headpiece showing the importance of designing hats with balanced trims.

- When designing a hat that is to match an outfit, pick one or more of the colours from within the outfit and echo these colours with carefully chosen trims. This will tie the hat and outfit together and create a symbiosis between them.

TOOLS AND MATERIALS

This chapter discusses the tools and materials needed to complete the different projects described in this book.

There are certain simple tools that are invaluable when making any kind of hat, such as pins and a needle, thread in a colour to match your fabric and a thimble. There are, however, different methods to use when making hats that require different equipment. If you are constructing flat pattern hats, there are certain materials that it is best to use, but the equipment needed can still be found in a normal sewing kit. Other millinery methods, such as blocking, are more specialist and require particular equipment to complete. The wooden blocks used for blocking create certain hat shapes, but these can be added to your collection as you need them and as you progress through the various techniques and styles of hat. Blocks are not needed for the first few chapters of this book and many different styles of hat can be made without blocking.

Fabric choice is so important in millinery. Most fabrics can be used if the right base construction method is chosen.

LEFT: **Tools of the trade: tape measure, ruler, household pins used for blocking, dressmaker's pins, bridal pins, glass-headed pins, toothbrush, clear adhesive, fabric scissors, fabric shears, pinking shears, paper scissors, snips, pliers, round nose jewellery pliers, pattern notcher, hat elastics, closed-ended thimble, millinery needles, tailor's chalk, beeswax.**

General Tools and Equipment

Beeswax

This is a vital tool for coating threads to stop them knotting or breaking, especially when sewing buckram or sinamay as these materials tend to shred threads.

Chalk

Tailor's chalk is useful for marking on felt or fabric.

Clear Adhesive

A clear glue that will dry as invisibly as possible is very useful for attaching flowers and other small trims. The glue is always covered, so it is not seen on the finished hat.

Cotton Tape (25mm Wide)

This is used for wrapping tightly around a blocked shape that needs to dry. This ensures the hood dries in the correct shape and the binding pushes the hood into the shape of the block. This method can leave binding marks that can be brushed out with a toothbrush.

Fabric Weight

This is a small fabric bag filled with uncooked rice used to weigh down a hood into indented details on a block, and is left in place until the hood is dry.

Hat Elastic with Metal Ends

This is a quick way to attach smaller hats to the head. The metal prongs have points that go through edging tape and are then hidden inside, leaving a neatly finished attaching method.

Hem Turner

This is a long metal stick with a rounded ball on one end and the other end squared with a hole in it. This is a very useful tool for turning sewn pieces the right side out, hiding the raw edges and untidy seams. The tool is most useful for pushing out the corners of the shape.

Invisible Thread

This is a clear plastic thread and is used when any other thread will show on the finished hat.

Needles in Different Sizes

Different-sized needles are used for different tasks. Sometimes a tiny, thin needle is needed to make invisible stitches in delicate fabric. At other times a long, strong milliner's needle is needed to sew through many layers or through a feather quill.

Paper

Use clean paper to cover the work table and to keep the hood clean whilst you stiffen it. There also needs to be clean paper or a table covering for the hood to sit on while it dries.

Pattern Notcher

This is a useful tool to use when creating patterns as the notches make the pattern pieces easier to match up when sewing the pieces together, especially on rounded or curved edges.

Pen with Disappearing Ink

This is useful for marking top fabrics as the ink will disappear over time.

Pins

Household pins are best for blocking as they are shorter, stronger and less likely to bend. Drawing pins are sometimes used when blocking, but they leave round indentations, especially in felt, and can leave rust-like marks on buckram and sinamay, so are not ideal for millinery use.

Dressmaking pins are thin, long and good for using with the finer fabrics used in millinery, such as silk.

Bridal pins are longer and thinner than household pins and are useful for pinning finer fabrics as they leave smaller holes.

Glass-headed pins are sturdy and strong and are useful for pinning buckram pieces together before sewing.

Pliers

A pair of heavy-duty piers are used for cutting millinery wire and flowers that have metal stems. Jewellery pliers with longer points are also useful when bending and shaping wire as they can produce neat corners.

Pressing Cloth

This is a piece of folded fabric that is stitched around the edge to form a tube and is used to protect the hands from heat when ironing into rounded or three-dimensional shapes.

Ruler

A ruler is used for measuring fabrics and trims, creating patterns and checking sizes before cutting.

Sandpaper

This can be used to smooth the cut edges of felt to give a softer finish.

Scalpel or Craft Knife

This is used for separating the crown from the brim after blocking hats.

It is helpful to have a collection of threads in different colours for making hats.

Scissors

Various types of scissors are useful for making millinery.

Snips are small scissors with sharp, fine points.

Fabric scissors are large, sharp scissors that should be used only on fabric to prevent them becoming blunt.

Paper scissors are cheap scissors used only for cutting paper – they will not be sharp enough to cut fabric neatly.

Buckram scissors are also cheap scissors, but need to be larger and stronger than paper scissors as buckram is tough to cut.

Tape Measure

A tape measure is an essential tool for any kind of making. It has many uses within the millinery process, from measuring the head to ensuring trims are in the right place on a finished hat.

Thimble

A thimble that fits well is an essential item in millinery as the fabrics used are tough to sew, and there are often several layers or stiffener to sew through. Thimbles are most useful when they are metal as these are the most sturdy. Thimbles are also used frequently when sewing together flat pattern hats made from buckram. It is useful to have a thimble that fits the index or forefinger as this tends to be the strongest. A thimble is also essential for blocking and is used for pushing the pins into the wooden blocks. For this purpose, a thimble that fits the middle finger is most useful. Closed-ended thimbles are the most commonly used thimbles, but some milliners do use open-ended ones.

Thin Shirring Elastic

This is used for tying around blocks that have string grooves in them to define this line as the blocked hat dries on the block.

Threads in Matching Colours

It useful to have thread that matches the fabric of the hat being made.

Toothbrush

A really basic cheap plastic toothbrush is very useful for brushing away chalk marks, raising the pile of felt hats and simply brushing the surface of hats clean of dust. The pile of felts can become flattened during blocking and brushing helps to counteract this. Fur felts with their longer pile can be brushed into a circular pattern. A toothbrush can also be used to brush the surface of felt to remove pinholes.

Wire

Cotton-covered wire can be purchased from millinery suppliers. Once sewn to the edge of hat pieces, thicker wire helps to keep the shape of the hat. Wire can also be used to strengthen other areas of the hat and to create head wires. Thinner wire can be used to give strength to trims.

Floristry wire is a fine wire that is used to give structure to flowers, feathers and other trimmings.

Tools for Blocking

Steamer

A hand-held or a Jiffy steamer® is useful for producing a continuous stream of steam, but a kettle is sufficient for most techniques where steam is needed.

Cling Film

This is used to cover wooden blocks so the water and moisture from the steam does not penetrate into the wood. Exposure to moisture shortens the life of blocks, so they need to be protected. Always replace cling film between blocking hats as the pinholes allow the water through to the block, and there may be residue of colour on the cling film that could transfer to a new hood.

Stiffener

Hoods need to be stiffened and dried before they are blocked. The stiffener will then help the hat to keep its shape.

Stiffener can be solvent-based or water-based. Water-based stiffeners are much less hazardous and give a similar effect to solvent-based stiffeners without significant hazards to the user's health. Water-based stiffeners can be used in usual workshop conditions, but solvent-based stiffeners must be used only in a working space with good ventilation and while wearing a mask at all times until the hood is dry.

Solvent-based straw stiffener is applied after the straw has been blocked but before it is removed from the block, whereas water-based stiffener can be painted onto the straw before blocking.

Brush

A 12mm painter's brush is useful for applying stiffeners.

Container

The container needs to be big enough to mix water-based stiffener with water. If using solvent-based stiffener, ensure the brush fits into the container and that the container will not melt when in contact with the chemicals.

Water Spray

A water spray is essential for misting the inside of the hood before steaming. This softens the material much more efficiently and makes the hood easier to block. Similarly, misting buckram, straw and sinamay with water before steaming helps to soften them too.

Plastic Bag with Tie Handles

This is useful when working with straw, sinamay and buckram. Mist the material with water and then fold and place inside the plastic bag. Tie the handles and leave for five minutes. The material will soften and will then be easier to work with.

Iron

A small travel iron with a pointed tip is useful as this will be able to manoeuvre around small areas.

Wooden millinery blocks are available in all sizes and shapes, but a few basics are all that are needed initially.

Millinery Blocks

Millinery blocks are wooden blocks in different shapes that are used to mould different materials into hat shapes. The material is stretched over the wooden block and then pinned to the block to keep the material in that shape whilst it dries. Millinery blocks are used when blocking either felt or straw.

The shape of the block is chosen carefully, or even specially commissioned, so that the finished hat is the correct shape. Blocks can be made to any shape, but the most common shape to begin with is the domed head-shaped block, which is very versatile. It gives the crown a smooth shape and can be used to make hats

such as bowler hats or a trilby. The blocks can be made to fit any specified head size, so if you are regularly making hats for people other than yourself, you will need a block in their head size or a range of sizes. The photograph shows examples of how different the shapes of the blocks can be.

Blocks are usually made by hand and are beautiful to display on a shelf when not in use. They can be expensive to buy, but suppliers have bundles that can be purchased at reasonable prices, and smaller blocks are often cheaper than larger ones. The suppliers list at the end of the book has suggestions of where you can source your blocks.

You will also need a stand on which to sit the block. This raises the block from the work surface and enables you to block to the bottom of the block. A stand will also allow the block to be turned round easily without having to pick the block up to work on it.

Blocks can also be made in sections that slide together so that they can be taken out of the finished hat in pieces. This allows the finished hats to be odd shapes and not symmetrical. These blocks are sometimes called puzzle blocks or five-piece blocks.

When working on a wooden block it is important to firstly cover the block with cling film before starting. This will protect the block from the water, steam and heat used in blocking, and will thus prolong the life of the block, preventing the wood from being damaged by moisture.

To attach the felt or straw hood to the block during blocking, it is necessary to pin into the wooden block. As the felt or straw hoods dry, they contract, so the pins will keep the hood in the blocked shape and they will not just slide off the block. The best pins to use for blocking are short, sturdy household pins or blocking pins (available from fabric shops and millinery suppliers). The pins are held between the thumb and forefinger and pushed in using the thimble on the middle finger. This is a technique that does need some practice to master, but it does make pinning easier. *See* Chapter 3 Techniques for full instructions on how to block.

It is best to leave the blocked shapes to dry naturally overnight or in a heat cupboard for an hour or so.

Hoods

Hoods is the collective term used to describe the prefabricated shapes that are the starting point when blocking hats. They are raw, head-shaped pieces of material from which the hats are made. Hoods can be made from either straw or felt and come in different basic shapes:

Cones have a deep crown but no distinct brim. Cones are shaped like flower pots and are used for making berets or hats with small brims, or hats with large crowns, such as top hats.

Capelines have shallow crowns and a large flat brim. They are larger than the cone and therefore more expensive. They are used to block larger-brimmed styles and are often cut into two pieces and used to block the crown and brim separately. It is possible to create a large-brimmed hat using a cone for the crown and a capeline for the brim.

Flares are A-shaped with a tall crown and a wide brim.

Felt Hoods

Felt hoods (or felts) can be made of wool or fur.

Wool felt hoods are the cheapest to buy, have a flat, well-matted surface and are available in a variety of weights and colours. They have a matt surface and can be thicker than fur felt, but they still make beautiful hats.

Fur felt hoods are similar to wool but are of better quality. They block more easily and have a softer pile due to having animal fur fibres within the felt. They are also more expensive than the wool felts but have a soft feel and a nice finished surface.

Millinery hoods are available in wool felt and fur felt.

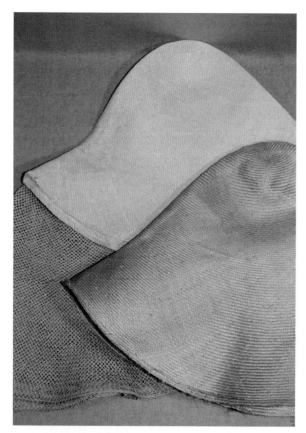

Straw hoods are available in a variety of surface finishes.

and can have many different weaves and patterns in their design. They can also be made from paper pulp.

Paribuntal hoods are made of a very fine and light straw that can be dyed a wide range of colours. The straw has a soft sheen when gently pressed and can be difficult to work with, so these hoods are not recommended for a first hat.

Parasisal hoods are a synthetic version of the paribuntal hoods, which makes them a cheaper alternative. These straw hoods can be bought in many different weaves and patterns, but can be quite thin and not very durable.

Peachbloom hoods have an added fur pile. The fur adds a very soft feel to the outside of the hood. Care needs to be taken with these hoods as adding stiffener to the fur side will ruin the surface.

Melusine hoods have a similar surface to peachbloom hoods but with a longer fur pile. They are significantly more expensive to buy.

Angora hoods are made of wool felt that has long angora hairs incorporated into the fabric.

Straw Hoods

Straw hoods can be made with different colours and kinds of straw, either natural or synthetic,

Panama hoods usually come in natural shades of cream and white. They are most often used for men's hats, but can also be used for ladies' boaters.

Wheat and double wheat hoods are made of a type of straw that is easy to work with and has a rough texture. They usually come in soft yellows or browns.

Paper straw hoods are made with a durable pulped paper and have an interesting texture.

Straw is a very different material to work with than felt and behaves in a very different way. When blocking with straw, work with the weave of the straw, pulling along the weave lines to flatten the straw to the block. Pulling downwards and out will not work with straw. (*See* Chapter 7 for advice on blocking with straw.)

Materials

The most common materials used in millinery can be both specialist and also more familiar fabrics that are used in dressmaking, crafting and interior design. The materials used most often are described below.

Buckram is a white woven fabric with glue embedded into it. Buckram is good for constructing flat pattern hats and can also be blocked and shaped with steam. It can be tough to work with, but creates lightweight millinery that hold their shape, and can successfully be made into either large-brimmed hats or sturdy bases for smaller hats, both of which can then be covered with top fabric.

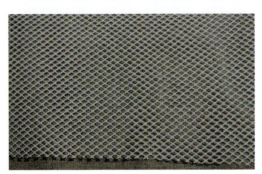

Paris net is an innovative white fabric that is a mesh embedded with glue, like buckram but with a much looser and wider diamond-shaped weave. Paris net is great to block with and, when used in layers in conjunction with buckram, can make some outrageous-sized brims that would be too heavy to support themselves if made in sinamay or buckram layers alone.

Sinamay is made from part of the *Musa textilis* plant (a type of banana plant) and has a natural straw-like texture. It is available in a rainbow of colours, prints and sparkly finishes. It can be bought by the metre and is suitable for blocking, though not an easy material to block on the first try! Once mastered, sinamay can create fantastic lightweight shapes and hats in rainbow colours and a variety of textures.

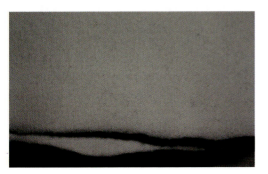

Felt is the easiest of the millinery materials to work with. It blocks beautifully and has a soft finish. Wool felts are the most basic and cheapest to buy and are available in cones, capelines and flare shapes. Felt can also be bought containing animal fur. These are collectively called fur felts but include peachblooms, velours, melusines and mohairs. They can be plain or printed and can range in price. Felt can be dyed and is available in a variety of colours.

Straw can be bought as cone or capeline hoods in many different colours, weights, textures and patterns. Straw requires some practice to block successfully. Like sinamay, it needs to be blocked working with the weave of the fabric.

Ice wool is a knitted fabric that is used to cover foundation materials such as buckram. Ice wool has an extra fluffy side and a flatter side, and is attached as a layer over the foundation material before covering with top fabric to avoid the texture of the foundation material showing through the top fabric on the finished hat.

Tarlatan is a lightweight cotton muslin with a stiffener as part of the fabric. It is used to cover foundation shapes.

Iron-on interfacing is a thin fabric with a series of tiny glue dots on one side. This is useful to use as a layer over base shapes before covering with top fabrics, and also as a strengthening layer for backing fabrics. It is ironed on and has an element of stretch, allowing it to cover shapes smoothly.

Transfer adhesive is a thin fabric-like layer of glue that has a paper backing and is ironed on to fabric. Two pieces of fabric can be bonded together using transfer adhesive. It is also useful for sticking fabrics to foundation shapes.

Fastenings

There are different methods for attaching hats and headpieces to the head. If the hat has a head fitting that fits around the head, it is likely to stay on the head, although hairgrips may need to be added to ensure it doesn't move. Headpieces can be smaller than the head fitting, so may sit on one part of the head or only perch on the head. These headpieces will need to be secured.

Different shaped hats require different fixing methods, including headbands, combs, hat elastics, clips and grips.

Metal headbands are the best to use as they are thin and can be easily disguised by covering the headband with the wearer's hair once it is on the head. Headbands can also be covered with ribbons or with strips of tulle that match the hair of the wearer.

Combs are available in different sizes and can be attached by sewing them to the underside of the headpiece. The comb will then secure the headpiece to the hair.

Hat elastics are used to attach smaller head-pieces. The elastic sits under the hair and is covered by the wearer's hair. Hat elastics have metal ends and can be pushed through peter-sham head fittings or edgings to secure them to the hat.

Clips and grips are for small headpieces or hair pieces. The grips are sewn directly to the underside of the headpiece and then can be slid into the hair.

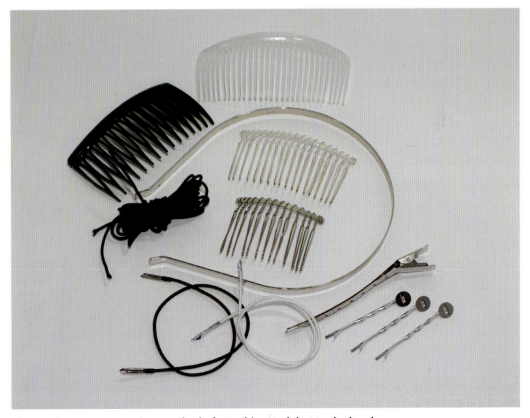

Choose the most appropriate method of attaching each hat to the head.

Making Your Own Flower Trims

Fabric Rose

Cut out a rectangle of fabric and fold in half with the wrong sides together. Measure a double length of matching thread. Knot the end.

Using a long running stitch, sew up one short end of the rectangle. Start sewing at the fold and work towards the open end.

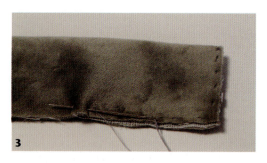

Sew along the long side of the rectangle about 0.5cm from the edge. This will sew the two open edges together.

Sew up the other short edge and cut the needle free from the thread.

Carefully gather the rectangle by pulling the thread. Do this evenly, being careful not to snap the thread.

Arrange the fabric with the gathered edge in the centre. Roll the edge tightly to begin with. Once you are happy with this shape, sew a few stitches through the fabric to secure it.

7

8

Continue to roll the rest of the flower around the centre piece to form the petals. You may need to tighten or loosen the thread as you roll. Secure with stitches as you go.

Once the flower is com-plete, tuck the final end under, secure with a few stitches and cut the thread. Rethread the needle with the gathering thread and secure this through the fabric with a few stitches. The flower is finished and ready to sew onto a hat.

Round blocked buckram disc headpiece with a fabric rose trim.

Fringe Flower

Fold a rectangle of fabric in half lengthways and use matching thread to sew along the open long side with a running stitch. Cut the rectangle into 1cm ribbons from the fold down to just above the line of stitches.

The ribbons will all move and give an organic effect similar to that seen naturally in flowers.

Leave the fabric flat without gathering the stitches. Roll the rectangle from one end, making securing stitches every few rolls.

Continue to roll the fabric the entire length of the rectangle and make securing stitches. Once the rectangle is all rolled and secured, tease the ribbons out to ensure they are not caught up on each other. The flower can then be stitched to the hat.

Gathered Fabric Flower

Fold a rectangle of fabric in half with wrong sides together.

With matching thread, sew five petal shapes in a continuous line of basic stitches. The fold of the fabric needs to be at the base of the petals.

Ruche the fabric by pulling carefully on the gathering thread to avoid snapping the thread. This will pull the petals into shape.

Knot the thread to stop it unravelling.

Secure the circle of petals together with a few stitches and add a button as a centrepiece.

Fabric flower trim made with hand-sewn fabric pieces, finished with buttons.

Fabric Leaves

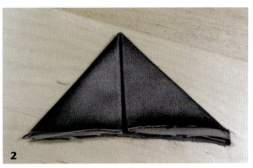

Fold a rectangle of fabric in half with the wrong sides together.

Then fold the fabric into a triangle by folding the top corners down diagonally to create a point. Pin the fabric to hold it together.

With matching thread, sew a line of running stitches along the base of the triangle and gather. This creates the point of the leaf.

Secure with a few stitches and knot the thread.

The finished leaf shape.

TECHNIQUES

Stiffening and Blocking

Hoods and fabrics are stiffened before being shaped into hat bases and flowers. This enables the stiffened material to hold the blocked shape once it dries. There are different kinds of stiffener available, both solvent-based and water-based. If you are using water-based felt stiffener there are fewer health and safety issues, but always ensure you are working in a safe manner and understand the products you are using.

You may need to factor in enough time in the hat-making process to add another layer of water-based stiffener to your hood. Making hats is not a simple or fast procedure and there are times in the process where the hat will need to dry, either in a heated cupboard for several hours or simply left out overnight. Ensure you are fully prepared before starting to block a hat. You will need to stiffen the hood before you can block it.

How to Stiffen and Block a Felt Hood

1 Ensure you are in a well-ventilated room when using either types of stiffener, but you will also need a fan vapour extractor if you are using solvent-based stiffener.
2 Cover the work surface with protective paper. This is not only to protect the table but also to stop your hat from picking up dirt. Ensure you are wearing an apron and gloves to protect your skin and clothes before you handle the stiffener.
3 Place a pin at the centre back point of a capeline hood and use this as a guide to covering the entire inside surface of the hood evenly. Be careful not to get the stiffener on the outside of the hood as this will leave a white residue that is difficult to remove.
4 Pour enough felt stiffener into a jam jar to roughly half fill the jar. Dip a brush into the liquid and scrape off the excess on the side of the jar.

LEFT: **Blocked felt perched crown with stylized brim and petersham trim.**

Blocking a straw hood.

5 Apply the stiffener to the inside of the crown of the hood using a small circular motion. Work the stiffener into the fibres of the felt. The felt will change colour as it gets wet, giving you a good indication if you miss any areas. The more stiffener you add to the hood, the harder it will dry. You do not want to add too much stiffener at this point. You can always add another layer later, if necessary.

6 Leave the hood to dry in a safe place out of the way or in a heated drying cupboard. This may take a couple of hours in a heat cupboard or overnight if left out in the air.

7 If you find that there is solvent-based stiffener on the outside of the hat once the hood is dry, this can be removed with a small amount of white spirit.

Trilby hat in blue felt with a hand-manipulated brim and a petersham band.

8 If you get some of the water-based stiffener on the outside of the hat, you will need to wait until it has dried completely before gently brushing the pile of the felt with a clean toothbrush, or a wire brush if necessary.

9 Once completely dry, the hood is ready to block.

10 Choose the crown block that you would like to use and ensure that the head size measurement is correct for the hat's intended wearer.

11 Cover the block completely with cling film. Ensure you smooth the film down carefully and do not let it bunch up or become bulky where it overlaps. You may need to use some tape to secure the film to the base of the block.

12 Turn on the steamer or kettle and wait for it to heat up.

13 Place the block onto a stand, as this will elevate the crown block up from the surface of the table to make it easier to work on.

14 Mark the centre back point by sewing a stitch of thread in a contrasting colour through the felt. Tie the ends of the threads in a loose knot so you can remove it easily when you are ready. Spray a small amount of water into the hood to dampen the crown and brim.

15 Whilst taking care not to burn yourself on the hot steam, place the hood over the steam outlet and turn it round slowly to ensure the steam softens the entire crown. You will see the steam creating droplets on the outside of the hood, and sometimes the steam will come right through the felt. Handle carefully!

16 You will notice how the felt becomes softer as the steam works into the fibres of the fabric. It will also get hotter and hotter as it gets softer, so be careful. Once the hood is soft and has been warmed by the steam, you are ready to block it. You will need

someone to help you with the initial blocking.

17 Hold the hood at the centre front and centre back whilst your helper holds the hood at the left side and right side. Place the hood onto the block with the centre back stitch indicator at the centre back of the block. Then simultaneously pull the hood down over the wooden block shape. It is very important to avoid stretching the felt unevenly, which is why this pull is done from the centre front and centre back points and the two centralside points at the same time – and this is why you need two pairs of hands to do it!

18 Once the hood is removed from the steam it will cool down very quickly, so it is important that you do this initial blocking fairly quickly. If you are not happy with the initial shape, you can take the hood off the block and put it back into the steam to begin the process again.

19 Once you are happy with the initial shape and the tip of the hood is following the shape of the tip of the block, you can begin to pin the felt to the block.

20 Always pin the four corner points first – centre front, centre back and the two central side points.

21 It can be helpful to create a loop of elastic to stretch around the base of the block to keep the hood in place whilst you pin, but this is not essential. This will also leave a mark on the felt that can be difficult to remove.

22 Gradually fill in the spaces between the four corner points with pins. You should do this by always working very evenly and adding the next pin on the opposite side of the block to the last pin.

23 Keep steaming the felt to soften areas and make them more workable. You can pull the felt taut and it will then stretch out evenly. This process will enable you to smooth out

24

any gathered felt and pin the felt to the exact shape of the wooden block.

24 Once pins have been added into all the gaps, leave the felt to dry overnight.

25 Always block down far enough on the block to allow a 1–2cm strip lower than the finished depth of your crown. This extra 1–2cm becomes an essential feature of the hat, as it gives a stand-up collar that enables you to attach the brim to a brim block and also to sew the brim and crown together.

26 Once the blocking is completed, the felt must be left on the block with all the pins left in until it is entirely dry.

27 If you need to remove the felt from the block or if you need to leave the hat and not finish it in one go, attach a head wire (*see* Working with Wire later in this chapter) to the inside of the crown with a tacking stitch to stop it from stretching. It would be wise to also create a head wire to tack into the brim to keep the head fitting correct here too.

28 Once the felt is dry, carefully mark the centre front, centre back and left and right side points with chalk. Remember to do this on both the inside and outside of the felt. Be careful when marking pale coloured felts; always use a pale-coloured chalk, or mark these points with a stitch of coloured thread if you think the chalk will leave a permanent mark.

29 Remove all the pins, discarding any that have bent out of shape.

33

36

35 Pin around the head fitting (inside the block) ensuring that you first pin the four corners and then that you pin evenly all around.

36 Pin the felt to the inside of the brim block so the felt is secure and it can be steamed and stretched over the brim block.

37 You can now use steam to soften the felt and pull out from the head fitting. Mould the felt to the shape of the brim block, curling the felt around the outer edge of the block and into the groove cut into the block. Pin in place all around the brim block.

38 If you find that the felt needs to be steamed further, use a clean, wet cloth dipped in a bowl of clean water to lay onto the felt and then iron with a hot iron. Do not have the steam setting on the iron turned on for this. This method is very effective and will allow the felt to be manipulated easily.

39 Allow to dry completely before removing the pins. Once the brim is dry (this could take several hours or even overnight if the felt has been heavily steamed), remove it carefully from the block and trim the felt along the line created by blocking into the groove on the block. This becomes the edge of the brim.

40 Again, store the brim on the brim block when you are not working on it to keep the shape.

30 Measure the required depth from the tip of the crown down towards the base of the block and mark this point all around. Then join these points with a chalk line. Measure down 1–2cm from these points and draw a second line all around on the felt crown.

31 Carefully remove the felt from the block and cut along the higher first-marked line. Be very careful not to stretch or crush the head fitting on either the crown or the brim.

32 Either return the crown to the block or tack in your head wire to keep the head fitting correct.

33 When the blocked crown shape is cut away from the brim, place it back over the crown block to avoid it stretching.

34 Place the remaining felt from the hood onto the chosen brim block. Ensure the head fitting is sitting around the lip of the block with the centre back mark on the centre back of the block.

37

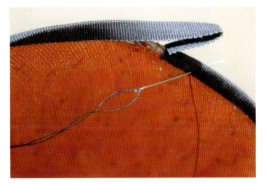

Slip Stitch. This is an invisible stitch used for sewing bindings such as petersham ribbon onto brims. The important thing with this stitch is to use the small stitch to catch a small amount of the fabric underneath, and then insert the longer stitch into the fold of the petersham.

A gold dupion silk-covered base with hand-sewn beading.

Stitches

There are certain stitches that are useful to know and use when making hats.

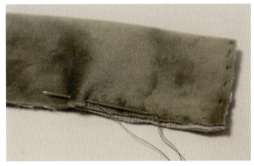

Running Stitch. This a very useful stitch that can be used to attach fabrics together or to gather fabric when making flowers.

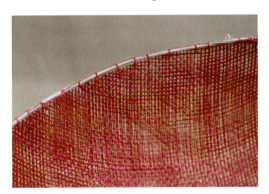

Wire Stitch. This stitch is used for oversewing wire to the edge of a brim or a headband. The wire should be held in place with the left thumb whilst the right hand sews towards it. The stitch consists of two small straight overstitches on top of each other that incorporate both the wire and the fabric, then a diagonal stitch away to move the stitch on.

Diagonal Running Stitch. This creates a diagonal stitch on the top side and a vertical one underneath. It is useful when sewing foundation materials such as ice wool onto a buckram base.

Open Backstitch. **This is similar to regular backstitch, except that the top stitch is smaller than the one underneath. This stitch is used when the stitches need to be invisible on the right side of the hat – make sure you use a thread colour that matches perfectly.**

Ladder Stitch. **This is a stitch that is simple to master and is used for attaching the crown to the brim when the hat is blocked in two pieces. It consists of stitches around 1cm long sewn onto alternate sides of the fabric.**

Tie Tacks. **This stitch is used for holding trims such as bows and veils on to hats. Make one stitch in exactly the right place and simply tie the loose ends of the stitch together at least three times before trimming the ends of the threads close to the knot.**

Working with Wire

You can use cotton-covered millinery wire to help the hat keep its shape. The wire is then covered with tarlatan before the edge is finished with either bias binding or self-covered with a folded edge. A head wire is a useful tool when making flat pattern hats and is easy to make. The head wire is fitted specifically to the wearer of the hat and is an integral part of making the crown fit the wearer perfectly. It is also part of the making process for the crown and brim. *See* Chapter 6 for instructions on using a head wire to draft the pattern for the beret.

To make a head wire you will need to measure the head that the hat is to fit (*see* How to Measure Head Sizes in the Introduction for instructions on how to measure the head). Once this measurement has been taken, add 8cm and then cut this length in cotton-covered millinery wire.

Straightening the Wire

Millinery wire is bought on a roll, so the wire is coiled like a spring. This coil needs to be removed from the wire before it can be attached to a hat, as the wire is used to follow and support the shape of the hat. If the wire is not straightened, it will pull the hat out of shape.

Flatten the coil and the spring out of the wire by folding the loop of wire back on itself against the direction of the coil.

Run your thumb against the curve of the wire to flatten it. This will make the circle of the wire bigger and flatter.

Sit the wire on a flat surface and continue to flatten it: where the wire hits the surface of the table, bend it up so that the end that is not sitting flat becomes flatter.

Do this gradually all the way around the wire circle.

The wire will eventually sit completely flat against the table and it is then much easier to work with. Mark a point on the wire 4cm from each cut end. Cross over the ends of the wire to form a circle, matching up the marked points.

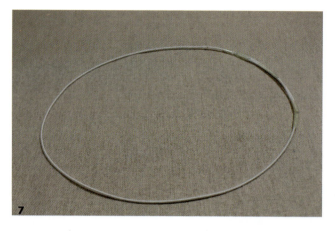

Use a small amount of tape to attach the wire together at this crossover point, wrapping the tape flat around both pieces of the wire from one end of the tape to the other. Use more tape to wrap around each of the raw ends, binding the ends to the wire circle. Be careful doing this as the cut ends can be very sharp. Try the circle of wire on the head. It may need to be manipulated into the correct shape, as some heads are naturally circular and some heads are more oval in shape. The shape of the head can also be affected by the hairstyle of the person, so ensure that the hair is being worn as it will be styled when the hat is on the head to ensure a good fit. The head wire can now be used to help create patterns for future hats.

Wiring the Edge

The next step is to wire the brim of the hat. Protect the head fitting of the hat by using the head wire described earlier to keep this delicate shape whilst you work on the outer edge of the brim.

1 Cut a piece of wire that is long enough to go around the brim and also cross over by 8cm at the centre back.
2 Flatten the wire as necessary and then, beginning at the centre back point, sew the

wire onto the brim using wire stitch (*see* the section on stitches in this chapter).

3 Once the wire is attached and you reach the centre back point once more, cross over the wires by the 3–4cm that is left over and secure with more wire stitch.

Covering the Wire with Petersham

1 To cover the wire and to give a neat finish to the brim of the hat, cut a length of 6mm wide petersham ribbon that matches the colour of the hat. The petersham should be long enough to cross over at the centre back point by 3cm.
2 Fold the petersham in half along its length and iron a crease in the ribbon.
3 To attach the petersham, fold over one raw edge by about 1cm and tuck this edge in between the brim and the tape. Sandwich the edge of the brim between the two halves of the petersham. This means that the crease in the centre of the ribbon sits

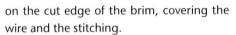

on the cut edge of the brim, covering the wire and the stitching.

4   Sew the petersham onto the edge of the brim using slip stitch (*see* the Stitches section in this chapter). As you sew, ensure that the petersham stays taut and is sitting flat on the edge of the brim.

5   When the petersham reaches the centre back point once more, fold the remaining tape back on itself and sew the two folded edges together. Lightly dampen the petersham all around the brim and, as it dries, it will shrink and tighten to ensure a flatter neater finish.

Attaching the Crown and Brim

Attach the brim to the crown by trimming down the head fitting lip on the brim to around 1cm and slotting the crown over this to sit on the brim. Ensure that the centre front and centre back lines match on the brim and crown. Sew the crown and brim together using ladder stitch (*see* the stitches section in this chapter).

The join can be covered by stitching a circle of 25mm-wide petersham ribbon into the head fitting. This will also act as a slight sizing adjustment and will make the hat more comfortable to wear. The hat then needs to be brushed very gently with a soft toothbrush to raise the flattened pile.

Finishing

The careful finishing of a hat is what makes the hat a desirable and beautiful accessory. No matter what the construction method, each hat takes a huge amount of time and skill to create, so the finishing must reflect this and make the hat worthy to be worn to any occasion. As many of the most spectacular hats are worn to special occasions, they are mini works of art and need to create a real wow factor.

Hats are multi-layered and need to be finished carefully to ensure these layers and the construction methods do not show on the final hat. The base materials may need to be covered with a layer of tarlatan or ice wool to stop the texture of the base showing through the top fabric. Care needs to be taken when using transfer adhesive as this can also be seen through some delicate top fabrics. Using glue to attach trims and feathers can be the only way to do this in some places and will generally give security to the trimmings, but the glue needs to be invisible or carefully hidden.

Stitches that are seen on the final hat are essential for attaching petersham ribbons and

MILLINERS' TIPS

As with any practical skills, there are certain ways of working within millinery that improve efficiency, safety and effectiveness. These are some of the methods and tips I have learned so far on my millinery journey.

- Always cover wooden blocks with a fresh layer of cling film before blocking. The wood needs to be completely covered to limit the amount of water and moisture that gets into the block. Cling film that has been used before is full of pinholes and will let the moisture through.
- Practise blocking using household pins and a thimble instead of drawing pins to cause less damage to the hoods and blocks.
- Always pin or block in opposites, starting with the 3, 6, 9 and 12 o'clock points on a clock face.
- Throw away broken pins or those that bend during blocking.
- Always use a thimble when blocking or sewing through bulky or tough materials.
- Be patient; always allow materials to dry properly after blocking.
- Stitches need to be perfect if they are seen; otherwise they need to be invisible or hidden.
- Buckram is a tough material that breaks and shreds sewing threads, but if the thread is coated with beeswax before stitching through the buckram, it is less likely to break.
- Cut millinery fabrics on the bias.
- Use the right material for the design – some designs lend themselves to certain materials that accentuate the design.
- Sinamay can irritate the skin, so always wear long sleeves when working with this material if you are sensitive to it.
- Attach top fabrics to base shapes by putting them on the bias of the base shape.
- Never use specialist fabric scissors to cut paper or buckram as they will blunt the scissors.
- Cover the sharp ends of wire after cutting or they can push through foundations and top fabrics.
- Allow glue enough time to set.
- Take your time!

certain trims. However, these stitches need to be neat and small – if they are seen, they need to be perfect. Otherwise they need to be hidden.

Always store hats in hat boxes when not in use.

Labelling Pattern Pieces

It is important to work in an organized and methodical manner within millinery. It is easy to lose trims or essential buttons or fastenings if they are not looked after. Often patterns will be reused again and again to make the same style in different fabrics, or simply to make another hat the same. For this reason it is helpful to copy the paper pattern pieces onto thin card or plastic so they last longer and the measurements are not altered by the pattern piece becoming rough around the edges or ripped.

Labelling pattern pieces is a useful habit to cultivate, as it will then be obvious which piece goes where. It also makes it easier to keep all the pattern pieces for one hat together, and if

This sinamay headpiece was blocked and shaped to fit the head and decorated with petersham and a curled quill.

you make variations of size or fit, you can easily identify which pieces to use. It is useful, too, if you need to recreate a hat you have already made to have all the pattern pieces together and clearly labelled.

As an example, the pattern piece for the sideband of a pillbox hat would be labelled as follows:

Pillbox
Sideband
50cm × 7.5cm
Overlap seam allowance: 8cm
Add seam allowance of 2cm to top and bottom edges

Balance Marks

These are marks made on the pattern pieces to help with constructing a flat pattern hat. These marks can be lined up on different pattern pieces and the seams will be easier to put together. The instructions for making the hats in Chapter 6 explain where to place them.

HEADPIECES –
SMALL, FUN, FAST

This chapter has two purposes: firstly, to provide an accessible introduction to hat making for beginners and secondly, to provide a fast means of making a new hat for an occasion that pops up at the last minute. For both first-time hat makers and more experienced makers short on time, small, fun, fast hats can be the perfect solution. They provide an opportunity to wear a hat created by you to show off your skills, finish off an outfit and ensure you feel special and unique at any event. There are ways that you can make a bespoke and original hat or headpiece to wear without needing lots of time, skill or experience.

The secret is that there are many really excellent ready-made ingredients that you can buy from millinery suppliers that allow you to trim a ready-made base to match your outfit or your mood. If you use a ready-made base, you can still choose colour, material and a fixing method, but it will arrive ready to use by mail order. All you need to do is trim it, secure it using the method that suits you best and you are ready to go and show off your creation!

The hats in this chapter can be adapted and customized using the millinery supplies you may already have or can purchase from suppliers. I have listed millinery suppliers at the end of this book and they all have online shops and offer mail order services.

LEFT: **Headpieces are small, fun and fast to make.**

Royal Blue Headpiece

This hat uses a royal blue sinamay base and is trimmed with feathers and a striped ribbon twisted into sculptural shapes.

You will need:

1 royal blue round sinamay base
1 metre of royal blue striped ribbon
1 feather bundle
1 circle of felt 1cm smaller in diameter than the base
hat elastic with metal ends
polystyrene head
thread that matches the blue base or invisible thread
2 needles, 1 strong and 1 fine
pins
metal thimble
snips

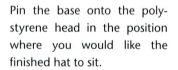

Gather the ribbon into two loops in the centre of the ribbon, leaving the cut ends free.

Place the loops of ribbon onto the base and wrap the cut ends around beneath the base. Cross them over and fold back around to the right side of the hat. Secure with a couple of pins through the ribbon and base.

Pin the base onto the poly-styrene head in the position where you would like the finished hat to sit.

Fold the remaining length of the ribbon into loops and arrange in and around the original loops. Make the loops different sizes but keep them on the top portion of the base. Play around with the place-ment of the loops until the hat looks balanced and interest-ing. Pin to secure.

Fold the ends of the ribbon under themselves and tuck under the loops already on the base to hide the cut ends.

Pin the sinamay base onto the polystyrene head in the posi-tion where you would like the finished hat to sit. Rearrange the loops as necessary until the design looks good on the base.

7

9

Remove the base from the polystyrene head. Secure the bows to the base with stitches in matching colour thread so the stitches are invisible.

8

Pin the base back onto the polystyrene head and place the feather bundle onto the hat to check where best to position it. Remove the base from the head and sew the feather bundle in place, ensuring that the tied ends of the bundle are hidden behind one of the loops. Sew through the tied bundle with a strong needle and thread, using a metal thimble to push the needle through the bundle. Remove any remaining pins.

Try the hat on and place a pin on either side of the hat where the natural side points are. These points correspond to where your ears are and marking them will ensure that the elastic sits behind your ears when the hat is worn. Turn the hat over and push the metal ends of the elastic through the edging tape; make a small hole in the tape first if necessary.

10

Once both ends of the elastic are attached, try on the hat to ensure it is in the right place and the right length. Sew around the small holes in the edging tape to secure.

11

Place the circle of felt on the underside of the hat. Secure it to the edging tape with a small slip stitch in a matching colour thread. This will line the hat and cover the stitches.

Chocolate Brown Hat

This hat uses a chocolate brown sinamay base that is trimmed with feathers, velvet ribbon and an oversized flower.

You will need:

1 chocolate brown oval sinamay base with a
   ribbon binding
3 goose feathers
1 small bundle of goose biot feathers
1 silk flower
1 circle of felt 1cm smaller in diameter than
   the base
hat elastic with metal ends
polystyrene head
thread that matches the feathers and flower
a strong needle and a metal thimble
pins
scissors
pliers

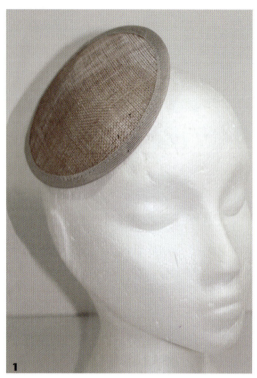

1

Pin the base onto the polystyrene head in the position where you would like the finished hat to sit.

2

Remove or trim any plastic stems that the flower may have, as the flower needs to sit flat on the base. If the stem has wire in it, use pliers to cut it.

3

4

5

Pin the flower to the base. Place the goose feathers onto the hat, tucking the ends of the feathers between the layers of petals to hide them. Pin into place on the petals.

Take the base off the polystyrene head and sew through the feathers and the flower petals to secure them to the base. Use a metal thimble to push the strong needle through the quill of each feather – this should be easier than you expect. Remove any pins.

Rearrange the flower petals to ensure they cover the ends of the feathers. Sew the flower securely to the base using small stitches in points around the flower, using matching colour thread.

Pin the base back onto the head and decide where the goose biot feather bundle best fits. Ensure that the ends of the bundle are securely tied together with thread and that they are hidden by the petals. The goose biots can be attached by sewing through the gathered quills and the base to secure them to the hat. Remove any remaining pins.

Try the hat on and place a pin on either side of the hat where the natural side points are. These points correspond to where your ears are and marking them will ensure that the elastic sits behind your ears when the hat is worn. Turn the hat over and push the metal ends of the elastic through the edging tape; make a small hole in the tape first if necessary. Once both ends of the elastic are attached, try on the hat to ensure it is in the right place and the right length. Sew around the small holes in the edging tape to secure.

Place the circle of felt on the base of the hat to cover the stitches. Secure it to the edging tape with a small slip stitch in a matching colour thread. This will line the hat and cover the stitches.

6

Plum Purple Hat

You will need:

1 plum purple teardrop-shaped sinamay
   base
3 plum coque feathers
3 large plum silk flowers
25cm of plum veiling
1 teardrop-shaped piece of felt 1cm smaller
   than the base
hat elastic with metal ends
polystyrene head
thread to match the veiling and flowers
needles
pins
snips and fabric scissors
clear crafting glue

LEFT: **This hat uses a teardrop-shaped base that is trimmed with flowers, feathers and veiling.**

Fold the veiling in half with the cut edges at the bottom and the finished edges at the sides.

Pin the base onto the polystyrene head in the position where you would like the finished hat to sit.

Gather the cut edges of the veiling into the centre and secure with a few stitches in matching colour thread.

4

Arrange the veiling on the base and pin. The veiling should be attached so the folded edge covers the pointed end of the teardrop base. Sew through the veiling and the base to attach it securely.

7

Dip the bottom 1cm of the feathers in the clear crafting glue. Place the feathers one by one into the gathered flowers and hold for thirty seconds to set the glue in place. Allow one feather to dry before adding the next one. Remove any remaining pins.

5

Cut down any stems on the large flowers and place them onto the base with their backs facing each other. This means that the petals all face outwards and the backs are covered by the petals from the other flowers. Pin in place, and then sew the flowers in place through the base. Remove the pins.

6

Trim the feathers to a length that allows them to stand about 3cm above the flowers. They can be different heights, but there must be three separate feathers. Arrange the feathers so they are spaced evenly over the top of the hat, as they tend to curl over. They will add height and movement to the hat.

8

Try the hat on and place a pin on either side of the hat where the natural side points are. These points correspond to where your ears are and marking them will ensure that the elastic sits behind your ears when the hat is worn. Turn the hat over and push the metal ends of the elastic through the edging tape; make a small hole in the tape first if necessary. Once both ends of the elastic are attached, try on the hat to ensure it is in the right place and the right length. Sew around the small holes in the edging tape to secure.

Place the circle of felt on the base of the hat to cover the stitches. Secure it to the edging tape with a small slip stitch in a matching colour thread. This will line the hat and cover the stitches.

Blue Hat with White Flowers

This hat is decorated with a trail of flowers over the surface of the hat. Tiny flowers are threaded onto thin plastic threads before they are attached.

1

Pin the base onto the polystyrene head in the position where you would like the finished hat to sit. Ensure that the join in the edging tape is in a position that will be covered by the flower decoration. On this hat, this is the 9 o'clock position. Make sure you keep the base in the same orientation when you remove it from the head to add the trims.

You will need:

1 blue saucer-shaped sinamay base
white goose biot feathers
small white silk flowers
1 bunch of white flowers
1 saucer-shaped piece of felt 1cm smaller than
   the base
hat elastic with metal ends

polystyrene head
thin plastic thread
blue and white thread
needles
pins
metal thimble
snips
pliers
clear crafting glue

Secure each flower with a tiny glue spot at the petal hole and the stem of the flower.

Cut the stems off the small flowers; you may need to use pliers if they are made with wire. Make a small hole in one of the outer petals with a pin. Push the plastic thread through the hole and make another pinhole in the petal opposite. This allows the flower to sit flat on the plastic thread.

Repeat until there are three plastic threads with flowers on each and allow to dry.

Attach the plastic threads to the hat with stitches that will be hidden by the flower decoration.

Attach the bunch of white flowers together; the wire stems will wind around each other quite securely. Arrange the flowers, hiding the stems and making sure they look pretty from every angle.

7

8

9

Sew the bunch of white flowers onto the base so that they cover the join in the edging tape and the stitches securing the plastic threads.

Dip the bottom 1cm of the goose biot feathers into the clear crafting glue and add them one by one to the hat. Tuck the feathers behind the white flowers and ensure that the ends of the feathers are hidden. Allow one feather to dry before adding the next one.

Arrange the feathers so they follow the shapes and lines of the hat. A mixture of straight, twisted and curled biots will add flair to the hat. Remove any remaining pins.

10

Try the hat on and place a pin on either side of the hat where the natural side points are. These points correspond to where your ears are and marking them will ensure that the elastic sits behind your ears when the hat is worn. Turn the hat over and push the metal ends of the elastic through the edging tape; make a small hole in the tape first if necessary. Once both ends of the elastic are attached, try on the hat to ensure it is in the right place and the right length. Sew around the small holes in the edging tape to secure.

Place the circle of felt on the base of the hat to cover the stitches. Secure it to the edging tape with a small slip stitch in a matching colour thread. This will line the hat and cover the stitches.

Blue Hat with Brooch

You will need:

1 blue sinamay base
1 stripped hackle feather fan
7 goose biot feathers curled and
    gathered into a bundle
1 blue flower
1 sparkly brooch
1 circle of felt 1cm smaller in diameter
    than the base
hat elastic with metal ends
polystyrene head
thread that matches the colour of the
    base and flower
needles
pins
scissors
pliers

This hat uses a blue base and is decorated with a blue flower, feather detail and a sparkly brooch.

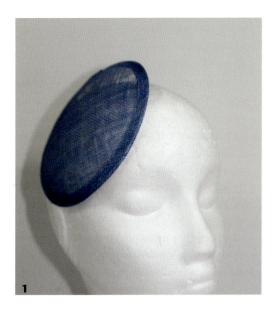

1

Place the base on the polystyrene head in the position where you would like the finished hat to sit.

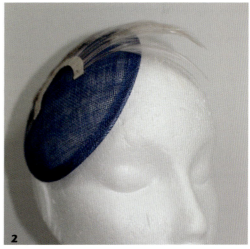

2

Pin the stripped hackle feather fan onto the hat base offset to one side. The curve of the feathers should follow the line of the head. The base of the fan can be sewn through easily to secure it to the hat base.

3

4

Cut off any stems from the flower so that it sits flat; you may need to use pliers if the flower has a wire stem. Attach the flower to the hat with pins through the outer petals, covering the ends of the hackle fan and towards the back of the hat base. Stitch the flower in place, hiding the stitches under the petals.

Add the goose biot feather bundle, hiding the ends between the flower petals and the base. Stitch through the feather quills and the base.

5

Remove the brooch pin from the back of the brooch using pliers. Place the brooch onto the base so the flower petals just overlap it.

Secure the brooch with stitches through the base. Place the stitches where they will not be seen and layer them on top of each other. Remove any remaining pins.

Try the hat on and place a pin on either side of the hat where the natural side points are. These points correspond to where your ears are and marking them will ensure that the elastic sits behind your ears when the hat is worn. Turn the hat over and push the metal ends of the elastic through the edging tape; make a small hole in the tape first if necessary. Once both ends of the elastic are attached, try on the hat to ensure it is in the right place and the right length. Sew around the small holes in the edging tape to secure.

Place the circle of felt on the base of the hat to cover the stitches. Secure it to the edging tape with a small slip stitch in a matching colour thread. This will line the hat and cover the stitches.

Plum-Coloured Hat with Petersham Ribbon Flower

You will need:

1 plum-coloured round sinamay base
10mm-wide petersham ribbon in
   tonal shades
1 circle of felt 1cm smaller in
   diameter than the base
hat elastic with metal ends
polystyrene head
matching thread and invisible thread
needles
pins
snips
pinking shears

This hat uses a plum-coloured round base and is decorated with a flower made from looped petersham ribbon.

1

2

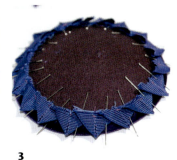

3

Cut the petersham ribbon into 3cm lengths with pinking shears to stop the petersham from fraying.

Cross over the cut ends of the petersham to form a triangle shape and sew a stitch through to secure.

Arrange the loops of ribbon in a circle at the edge of the base and use pins to keep them in place. Tuck the ends under so the next petals overlap and hide them. Stitch each petal securely to the base.

4

Add the next layer of petals, arranging them so the points of the second layer of petals lie between the points of the first layer. Secure with pins before sewing to the base.

5

6

Continue to add layers of petals in the same way, gradually making the circles smaller.

Layering the colours of the petals gives a really pretty effect.

7

8

For the centre of the flower, cut five more peter-sham strips and fold them into triangles. Stitch through to hold the shape.

Place two triangles with their folded sides together. Use backstitch to sew from the outer point to the centre of the longest side. Secure the thread and cut. Continue adding the trian-gles in the same way and sewing them from the outer point to the centre line.

Once all the triangles have been added, sew up the final edge and the central flower is complete. Sew onto the centre of the flower, taking care to keep the stitches small. Remove any remaining pins.

9

Try the hat on and place a pin on either side of the hat where the natural side points are. These points correspond to where your ears are and marking them will ensure that the elastic sits behind your ears when the hat is worn. Turn the hat over and push the metal ends of the elastic through the edging tape; make a small hole in the tape first if necessary. Once both ends of the elastic are attached, try on the hat to ensure it is in the right place and the right length. Sew around the small holes in the edging tape to secure.

Place the circle of felt on the base of the hat to cover the stitches. Secure it to the edging tape with a small slip stitch in a matching colour thread. This will line the hat and cover the stitches.

10

1950s-INSPIRED HATS

The hats in this chapter are designed to echo the style, shapes and colours of the 1950s. Historical eras and 'vintage' styles are an exciting fashion influence and can be seen in all areas of fashion, hair, make-up, accessories and interiors. There are many different popular decades that are recreated, and most of them have a handmade feel and highlight beautiful design and artisan creators.

The hats in this chapter take on a few more ideas following on from the designs in Chapter 4. They use some of the excellent ready-to-use ingredients from the millinery suppliers and customize them to echo the theme and personalize the finished hats.

Disc Headpiece with Flower

This hat starts as a 15cm sinamay disc and becomes an O-shaped headpiece.

You will need:

15cm sinamay disc
petersham ribbon in both 15mm and 25mm widths
flower
vintage buttons

thread that matches the colour of the trims
needles
pins
snips
tape measure
pen
iron

LEFT: **A range of 1950s-inspired hats.**

This will also remove the plastic ring that reinforces the edge of the sinamay. Keep this ring safe.

Cut the threads that hold the tape to the edge of the sinamay disc.

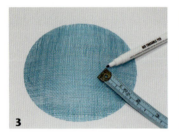

Measure the sinamay disc from the outer edge towards the middle and mark points all the way round the disc 4cm from the edge. Connect the marks to form a smaller circle.

Cut this small circle out from the centre of the sinamay disc.

Measure the circumference of the outer edge of the disc and add 2cm. Cut a corresponding length of the 25mm petersham ribbon. Fold the petersham ribbon in half lengthwise and pinch with your fingers to crease.

Iron the petersham using a medium heat and curve the petersham into a C shape. Do this by holding the iron on one end of the petersham and pulling the other end towards you as you run the iron along the length of the petersham.

7

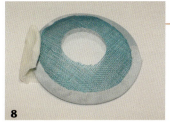

8

9

Pin the end of the petersham to the outer edge of the sinamay disc, pulling as you pin to stretch it slightly. Sew the petersham onto the sinamay disc all the way round, using a single thread in a matching colour and a fine needle so that it makes small holes.

Using a damp cloth, wet the petersham. As the petersham dries, it will shrink slightly and fit more tightly to the disc. Set aside to dry.

Measure the circumference of the central hole in the sinamay disc and add 2cm. Cut a corresponding length of the 15mm petersham. Curve the petersham (*see* step 6) and sew to the edge of the hole (*see* step 7). Ensure that the join in this piece of petersham lines up with the join in the petersham attached to the outer edge. Wet the petersham (see step 8) and then set the disc aside to dry.

Sew the flower onto the disc to cover the joins in the petersham. Hide the stitches on the underside by keeping them as small as possible. Sew the vintage buttons into the centre of the flower and onto the disc.

10

Joined Discs Headpiece with Flowers and Veiling

You will need:

2 coral sinamay discs
flowers
veiling
polystyrene head
invisible thread
needles
pins
snips
pliers

This headpiece is made by joining sinamay discs, which are then trimmed with veiling and flowers.

1

Overlap the two discs and pin into place. Use invisible thread to join the discs securely together. This will ensure that the stitches are not seen.

2

Drape the veiling over the polystyrene head and pin into place.

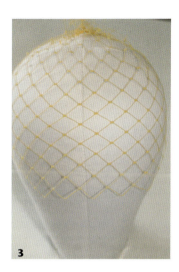

Place the discs on top of the veiling and pin the veil to the discs.

Remove the discs from the polystyrene head and place them upside down on the table. Using invisible thread, sew the veiling to the discs. Ensure that the gathered veiling is hidden from view under the discs.

Gather the excess veiling up on to the top of the head to make it sit flat around the face. The gathered veiling should be in the area that will be covered by the sinamay discs.

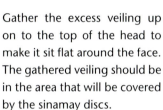

Arrange the flowers back to back on the disc so the stems are hidden. The stems of the flowers may be too long, so may need to be cut down using pliers.

Sew the flowers securely onto the sinamay disc with invisible thread.

Flower Headpiece

You will need:

cotton-covered millinery wire
velvet ribbon in contrasting colours
vintage-style buttons
veiling
a wooden or polystyrene head block
thread that matches the colour of the
    ribbons and the veiling
needle
pins
thimble
snips
pliers
sticky tape

This velvet headband is made from cotton-covered millinery wire and shaped to fit the head. It has a veiling base and a handmade velvet ribbon flower trim.

1

Flatten the wire (*see* Working with Wire in Chapter 3). Begin to fold the wire to form the sides of the headband. Start with the raw end in the middle of the head so that the joins in the wire are not at the ends of the headband. Fold the wire over the head several times until you have four points.

Gather the wire points and split them into two pieces of wire that are anchored at the points. Tape the raw edges to the wire with a small amount of sticky tape. Manipulate the wire until it fits snugly around the head similar to an Alice band.

2

3

Wrap the velvet ribbon around the wire. Begin at one of the points and tuck the raw edge of the ribbon under the layers of the wrapped ribbon. Overlap the edge of the point slightly as this will be sewn later to secure it.

Wrap the entire length of the wire, travelling along one side and then back along the other side.

4

Finish by folding the end of the ribbon under itself and sew to the ribbon underneath with tiny stitches.

Sew the ends of the ribbon with matching colour thread to secure at both points.

5

Check the headband fits the head and adjust if necessary.

To make the flowers: Cut the ribbon into six 6cm strips for each flower. Fold the ribbon in half (wrong sides together) and sew along the open end. Use a matching colour thread and ensure there is a secure knot that the end.

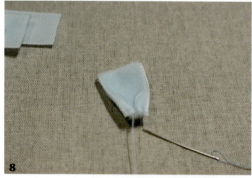

Gather the stitches to ruffle the ribbon into a petal. Fold the petal in half and sew through the gathered end to keep the shape. Secure the thread and cut.

Repeat this to make all five petals.

Sew the petals together through the corners of the gathered edges. Ensure each petal is secure before knotting the thread.

Turn the flower over and fold each petal inside out. This puts the stitches on the back of the flower. Cut a small square of velvet ribbon and sew it to the back of the flower. Use this as a secure base on which to sew a button to form the centre of the flower.

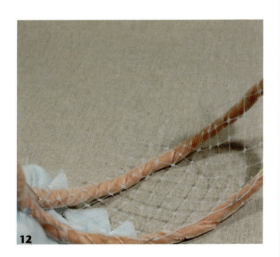

Sew the flowers to the wire headband with thread that matches the colour of the flowers. Pin the veiling to the underside of the head-band, ensuring that the finished edge of the veiling is facing the front of the headband. Pin all the way down the front edge first. Check that the veiling will not be visible once the headband is on the head.

Sew the veiling to the headband using thread that matches the veiling. Sew through the spots on the veiling and secure to the velvet ribbon on the headband. Keep the stitches small and neat.

FLAT PATTERN HATS

Flat pattern hats are those that are made by using pattern pieces to cut out pieces of fabric that are then constructed into hats. The fabric can have a layer of interfacing or canvas sandwiched inside to give it strength and structure; or the pieces can be cut from a material such as millinery buckram that is embedded with glue and has a rigidity of its own. Hats constructed from buckram pieces make a base shape that then needs to be wired for strength and covered in top fabric. There often needs to be a layer of interfacing between the buckram and the top fabric to stop the wire or the texture of the buckram from showing though the top fabric. This chapter will show how to use these construction techniques.

Flat pattern hats can be made either by hand or by using a sewing machine. The style of the hat will define whether you can use a sewing machine or if hand sewing is more appropriate. Flat pattern hats constructed from buckram often do not fit under the sewing machine foot, especially when the shape has been wired. This would mean that the shape would be squashed by using a sewing machine, so sewing by hand is sometimes necessary.

It is important when making flat pattern hats that the pattern pieces are measured accurately, have balance marks and are labelled

carefully (see Chapter 3), so that they do not get confused and the pieces fit together easily and as they should. It is therefore useful to label each pattern piece for each project you make. This makes it easier to keep all the pattern pieces for one hat together, and if you make variations of size or fit, you can easily identify the pattern pieces required. Having all the pattern pieces together and clearly labelled is also useful if you need to recreate a hat you have already made.

As an example, the pattern piece for the sideband of a pillbox hat would be labelled as follows:

- Pillbox
- Sideband
- 50cm x 7.5cm
- Overlap seam allowance 8cm
- Add seam allowance of 2cm to top and bottom edges

Example of a pillbox hat in purple with a handmade flower trim.

LEFT: **Flat pattern hats can be very diverse. Using the same techniques can produce different styles of hats.**

Berets are versatile hats and can be made from all kinds of fabrics.

Berets

The beret is an instantly recognizable shape. It is a very versatile hat and is stylish as well as being practical. The beret complements many different kinds of outfit and can be either daywear or made in a finer fabric for a more sophisticated evening look. Berets can be made in any colour and can be plain, textured, embroidered or appliquéd.

Berets can be different sizes and shapes, and this means that they can be worn in a variety of ways. The size of the sideband and the tip can be altered to give a very different shape to the finished beret. The pieces can also be topstitched, which gives structure to the fabric and again alters the way in which the beret sits on the head. For example, berets can be worn at a rakish angle or pulled down to tuck in the ears on a cold day.

Constructed Beret

The simple beret pattern begins with a head wire that fits snugly around the head of the wearer. Ensure the head wire fits the wearer comfortably without being too tight. We all have heads that are slightly different shapes: some are more rounded and some are more oval. The perfectly circular head wire will need to be squashed into more of an oval shape to fit the wearer. Working with Wire in Chapter 3 explains how to create a head wire.

Cut pattern paper into approximately a 30cm square and fold in half, and then again into quarters. The creases made will show the centre of the square. Mark this point as the centre point.

You will need:

pattern paper

pencil

head wire

velvet top fabric for beret and headband

lining fabric

thread that matches the colour of the fabric

needle and sewing machine

pins

paper and fabric scissors

ruler

iron

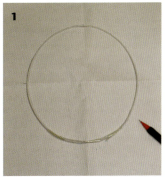

Place the head wire onto the pattern paper with the centre point of the paper in the centre of the head wire. Draw around the head wire onto the pattern paper and remove the head wire. This is the head fitting line.

The constructed beret is made with a cotton velvet in a bold colour to brighten up winter days.

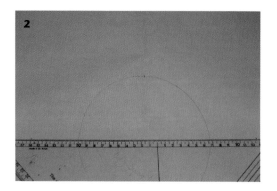

Measure inside this line 1cm and draw another circle inside the head fitting line at that point. This is the seam allowance, which allows the edge to be finished.

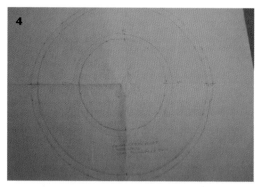

Mark balance marks on the head fitting line – I suggest using the points of the clock at 3, 6, 9 and 12 o'clock. These are very useful reference points in millinery. Measure out and mark further points at equal distances all the way around the head fitting line. Join these points to create the sideband of the beret. This can be as deep or shallow as you like.

Measure out 1cm from the sideband line and draw another circle 1cm bigger than the sideband line. This is the seam allowance for sewing the pieces together. You have now created the sideband pattern piece; label it clearly. Cut out the sideband pattern piece and lay it on the paper. Draw around the outer edge to form the pattern piece for the tip (the uppermost part of the crown). Add 2cm to the head fitting measurement and draw a rectangle with this measurement as the longest side and 10cm wide. This is the stand pattern and will be sewn to the head fitting and go around the head. Do not forget to add the balance marks to these new pieces.

Place the paper pattern pieces onto the top fabric and pin securely. Cut the pieces out. You will also need to cut a tip piece from the lining fabric. Transfer the balance marks to both the top fabric and the lining fabric.

Place the tip and the sideband right side together and pin around the outside edge. Sew the pieces together around this outside edge.

Create a binding using the stand piece. Fold the stand piece in half and then fold each raw edge in up to the central fold line. Press this binding flat with a cool iron.

Securely pin the binding onto the seam allowance around the inside edge of the sideband and then sew them together.

Place the lining into the hat with the right side facing upwards. Use the balance marks to match up the lining to the seam allowance on the beret. Fold the binding over this raw seam and pin through the beret seam, the lining and

Fold the binding in half and fold in the raw edge to encase the seam allowance of the beret. Press the binding so it sits neatly and the raw edge is pressed flat inside the binding.

the binding. This tidies the seam and finishes the edge of the beret.

Hand sew the binding through the lining to the beret seam. These stitches will not show on the outside of the hat. The finished beret is now ready to wear.

Sectional Beret

The sectional beret is assembled in a similar way to the constructed beret and is adapted from the same pattern. The tip of the sectional beret is split into equal sections and constructed before the beret is sewn together.

You will need:

pattern paper
pencil
the tip pattern from the constructed beret
fleece top fabric for beret and headband
lining fabric (if desired)
a button to trim
thread that matches the colour of the fabric
thread in a contrasting colour for tacking
needle and sewing machine
pins
paper and fabric scissors
ruler
iron
tailor's chalk

The sectional beret is made using fleece fabric for warmth and practicality.

Fold the tip pattern piece into eight sections. Cut along the fold lines and use this to create the sections for the beret.

Each triangular section will need to have a 1cm seam allowance added to the longer sides. Add a 6cm seam allowance to the shorter edge. This adds the sideband to the sections.

Cut out the sections in the fleece fabric and pin together. Transfer the balance marks to the tip: these are 3, 6, 9 and 12 o'clock.

Tack the sections together in groups of four with a contrasting thread. As there will be eight points joining in the centre, this helps the joins to be neat and accurate.

You now have two semicircles, each containing four triangles.

Put the two semicircles right sides together, making sure they sit neatly and the points are aligned.

Sew the sections together on the sewing machine. Keep the seam allowance at 1cm.

This will create the circular tip of the sectional beret.

Press the sections and either trim back or overlock the seams.

For the sideband, measure a rectangle that is the same length as the head fitting plus 3cm for seam allowances. The rectangle should be 7cm wide – this allows 6cm for the sideband and a 1cm seam allowance.

Transfer the balance marks to the sideband using tailor's chalk. Sew up the centre back of the rectangle to make it into a loop.

Leave the sideband flat and line up the balance marks on the tip to those on one side of the sideband.

13

14

15

The tip will be larger than the sideband, so ease the extra fabric into each section by dividing it into equal sections and pinning it equally in each section of the sideband, right sides together. This will give a gathered effect on the finished beret.

Sew the sideband to the tip and remove the pins.

Fold the sideband in half to the inside, tuck the 1cm seam allowance under and pin.

16

17

Use a hand slip stitch to attach the sideband to the hat. This encases the raw edge of the gathered fabric and finishes the beret neatly. Fleece does not fray, so there is no need to line the beret in this fabric. If making the beret in another fabric, the beret will need to be lined to finish the inside.

Finish the beret with a button or a pom-pom that sits at the point where all the sections join on the top.

Shaped Buckram Hats

Buckram is a woven material that is used specifically for millinery. It has glue embedded into it, which makes it very versatile when being used in flat pattern form as here, but it can also be blocked. Using the buckram to make flat pattern hats creates a strong and solid base that can be covered in any top fabric. *See* Chapter 6 for more information about using buckram when creating blocked hats.

Three-Section Constructed Buckram Headpiece

This headpiece is constructed in three sections that are covered before being attached together to create the final hat. The shape for this headpiece was inspired by an art deco-style mirror and echoes the shapes made popular in this era.

The shaped buckram headpiece has wire sewn around each of the pieces, so that when the headpiece is finished, it can be moulded to follow the shape of the head.

Buckram headpiece constructed in three pieces and covered with silk.

You will need:

buckram
pencil
top fabric in two different colours to cover the
    buckram and to make bias binding
ice wool
feather trim
polystyrene head

matching thread
needles and/or sewing machine
pins
metal thimble
millinery wire
buckram scissors
pliers to cut wire
iron
tailor's chalk

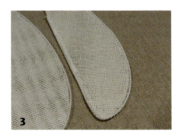

The shape of this headpiece is teardrop. Cut out two pieces of buckram the same size and shape. Iron the two pieces together – spray lightly with water and use the steam setting on the iron to fuse the layers together.

Cut one of the pieces in half lengthways. Use the buckram pieces as a template to cut pieces of wire that encircle each piece. Flatten the wire (*see* Working with Wire in Chapter 3) and then bend the wire so that it follows the shape of the buckram.

Sew the wire to the edge of the buckram shapes, either by hand using a wire stitch or by using a wide zigzag stitch on a sewing machine.

Cover each of the buckram pieces with ice wool. Stitch the ice wool in place to keep it flat.

Decide on which colour of top fabric to use to cover the larger buckram piece and which will be used to cover the smaller pieces.

Curve the pieces of buckram to the desired final shape by trying them against the polystyrene head.

Place the larger buckram piece on the top fabric and draw around it with tailor's chalk, ensuring that there is enough seam allowance to cover the curved shape. Cut out two pieces the same.

Stretch the top fabric over the shape and sew near to the edge to secure. Trim the seam allowance back once the top piece is secure.

Measure the outside length of the buckram piece and cut a bias strip of top fabric of the same length to fold into bias binding.

To join together smaller strips. place the two ends right sides together at right angles to each other. Fold the top piece up so that the two pieces of binding become one continuous length. Press with the iron and then unfold.

Draw along this fold line with tailor's chalk. Pin the binding together and sew along this diagonal line. Trim off the excess binding.

Pin the bias binding to the edge of the buckram piece, covering the raw edges of the top and lining fabrics.

Cover the two smaller pieces of buckram with the contrasting top fabric in the same way.

Create bias binding in the same way as for the larger buckram piece. Curve the three sections to the head.

Pin the smaller buckram sections to the central piece and sew through with large stitches to secure.

Now sew the bias binding onto the curved side of the section.

Once both the sections are bound, the hat construction is completed.

Finally, add trims to the finished hat. The trims used here are a burnt ostrich feather, curved to follow the shape of the head, and a bundle of three goose biots in a matching colour, each curled to complement the shape of the hat.

Pillbox Hats

A pillbox hat is understated, but has a simple elegance and is easy to wear. The definition of a pillbox shape is a hat that has a sideband with straight sides and a flat top. The sideband can vary in depth and the hat itself can be large or small. A pillbox hat can be round or oval in shape. The finished hat can sit at the back, on the top or on the side of the head, or can perch more towards the front.

Pillbox hats are constructed from buckram pieces that are wired for support and covered with foundation materials and a layer of top fabric. The hat is then trimmed.

The first step when making the pillbox is to make the pattern for the sideband:

- Decide where the hat will sit on the head and then measure the head at that point for the circumference of the hat. This measurement is the length of the sideband. Add 8cm to the length of the sideband; this is the seam allowance and enables the sideband to be attached to the top of the hat.

- Decide how tall the pillbox needs to be – this can be shallow or deep depending on the design of the hat, although the hat needs to be deep enough to sit comfortably on the head. Use a tape measure to decide the right height. This measurement is the height of the sideband.

Brown Wool Pillbox

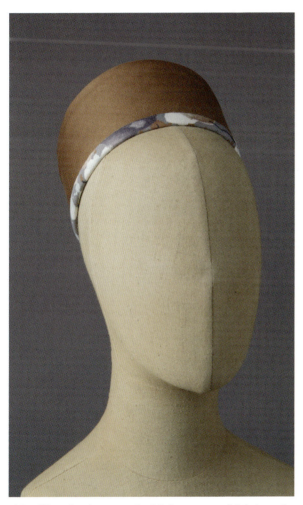

This pillbox hat is covered with brown wool fabric and has a patterned bias strip around the head fitting.

You will need:

pillbox sideband pattern

buckram

top fabric, lining fabric and contrast fabric

tarlatan

ice wool

matching thread

needle and sewing machine

pins

thimble

millinery wire

beeswax

chalk

fabric scissors and buckram scissors

iron

Fuse two layers of buckram together for added strength by spraying the buckram lightly with water before ironing evenly all over. Leave to cool.

1

Trim the raw and uneven edges from the buck-ram once it is cool.

Draw around the sideband pattern piece on the buckram. Include an extra 4cm on top of the head measurement for the securing overlap.

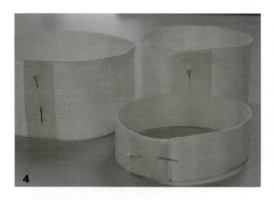

Create a ring with the buckram lining up the overlap line. Use a strong pin to secure.

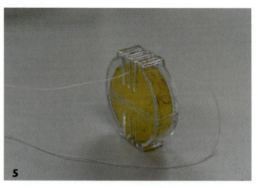

Coat your thread with beeswax. This will strengthen it and avoid it breaking when being passed through the buckram.

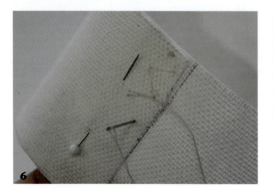

Sew the overlap from top to bottom using a large zigzag stitch.

Wire the edge of the sideband with millinery wire as described in Wiring the Edge in Chapter 3.

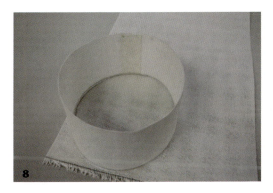

Place the joined sideband onto another piece of buckram and draw around the inside edge, using it as a template to create the tip of the pillbox.

Cut out and wire the edge of the tip. Pin the tip to the sideband and use an overstitch to attach the tip to the sideband.

Cut out a tip and sideband in tarlatan and use these to cover the pillbox shape to smooth the surface of the buckram. Sew to secure.

Place the sideband pattern on the top fabric on the bias. Draw around the pattern with tailor's chalk, adding a 2cm seam allowance along the long sides of the pattern. The sideband pattern already incorporates a seam allowance at the short ends where they overlap. Place the buckram base upside down on the top fabric and draw around it to create a tip in the top fabric. Add a 2cm seam allowance all round. Carefully cut out the pattern pieces. Mark and cut tip and sideband pieces from the lining fabric in the same way.

Carefully snip into the seam allowance to the chalk line to form tabs. Place the top fabric tip onto the buckram pillbox base.

Fold the tabs down the walls of the sideband and pin to secure, placing the pins at the 3, 6, 9 and 12 o'clock positions, and smooth the tip fabric out over the buckram base.

Cover the sideband with ice wool and sew the centre back seam. Use large stitches to secure the ice wool through the sideband.

Fold over the seam allowance at the top of the sideband and press with an iron to create a neat crease.

Placing the right side of the top fabric sideband piece against the buckram shape, smooth the fabric and pin at the centre back.

Carefully wriggle the side-band top fabric over the buckram

shape, matching the folded edge of the sideband to the tip. Leave the bottom sideband edge free.

Use tailor's chalk to draw a line where the fabric overlaps and sew this seam on a sewing machine. Trim the excess fabric from the centre back seam.

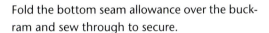

Fold the bottom seam allowance over the buckram and sew through to secure.

Cut a strip of contrast fabric on the bias. Create bias binding by folding the fabric in half and pressing. Then unfold it and fold each edge into the middle. Press again.

Unfold the bias binding and wrap around the bottom edge of the sideband. Pin in place and sew the centre back seam. Then sew around the sideband going through the buckram base.

To make the lining, sew the centre back seam of the sideband and then sew the sideband and tip lining pieces together. Pin in place on the hat and sew to secure.

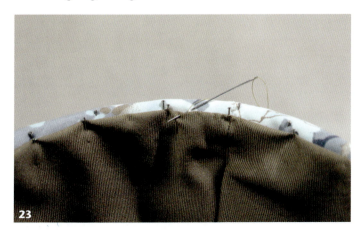

Finally, fold the bias binding over the edge of the sideband, covering the previous stitches. Fold in the raw edge of the binding and slip stitch.

BLOCKED HATS

Blocking is an art form and a rewarding technique that produces beautiful and sculptural hats. It involves stretching a material over a shaped wooden hat block and pinning it in place to dry. The block can be a crown or a brim, a plain head shape, a simple angled shape or a fancy sculptural shape depending on the block used.

A hat can be blocked in two pieces – a crown and a separate brim – or one block can produce a whole hat where the crown and brim are blocked together over an all-in-one block. There are also hat styles that have a crown but no brim. The material used for blocking has a stiffener or sizing within or painted onto the fabric. This enables the material to take the shape of the block once the glue dries.

Blocking can be both relaxing and rewarding. It does require some practice of the technique and patience is needed, along with some brute strength both to pull the material into shape and to push the pins into the wood.

Blocking creates lightweight shapes that can either be base shapes to be covered in top fabric or final shapes that just need to be finished and trimmed; but most blocked hats need to be reinforced with cotton-covered millinery wire to help to support the shape.

LEFT: **A selection of the blocked hats described in this chapter.**

Pink and green sinamay hat trimmed with feathers.

Any of the main millinery fabrics – felt, sinamay, straw and buckram – can be blocked. Each fabric has its limitations and there are shapes that work better in some materials than others (*see* Chapter 2). Blocked buckram shapes create a base layer that needs to be finished by covering with a flat fabric, whilst shapes blocked in straw, sinamay and felt can be used without covering.

Sinamay Hat with Feather Trim

Sinamay is a straw-like woven material that is made with fibres from the Musa textilis plant (which is similar to the banana plant), indigenous to the Philippines. The fibres are woven into an open weave fabric that can be dyed to any colour and shade.

Sinamay is very versatile: different threads and glitter can be added to the weave, it can be printed onto and can have decorative patterns woven into it. Sinamay can be blocked like straw and felt and has glue infused into it to keep the blocked shapes once dry.

Sinamay can be quite sharp when it is cut and can easily weaken and break threads when you sew through it. Sinamay can also be irritating to

You will need:

saucer block
plain sinamay in bright pink
basket-weave sinamay in lime green
lime-green petersham ribbon
shaped trims for decoration
polystyrene head
threads that match the colours of the sinamay
needle
pins
cotton-covered millinery wire
beeswax
cling film
water spray
plastic bag
snips and buckram scissors
clear crafting glue
headband or comb

the skin, so long sleeves should be worn when blocking and working with it.

It is a lightweight material that is self-supporting, which means large shapes can be made without becoming too heavy to wear. It can be used as the finished surface of the hat without needing to be covered with any top fabric, so can be made into many different shapes and sizes of hats.

Block the pink sinamay over the saucer block. Use the rounded wooden dome to make the shape in which the head will sit. Allow to dry with the rounded dome in place.

1

Check the shaping of the sinamay by placing it on the polystyrene head.

Trim the sinamay down evenly to the highest desired level all the way around.

Cut the front of the sinamay down to make the shape asymmetric.

Spray the green sinamay with water and fold into four. Place in a plastic bag and tie the handles.

Cover the block with fresh cling film and block the green sinamay over the saucer block, using the rounded wooden dome to create the indentation for the head.

Allow to dry with the rounded dome in place.

Take the pins out of the sinamay and remove from the block. The cling film can be discarded.

The blocked sinamay layer should look like this.

Layer the pink sinamay inside the green sinamay and pin together.

Flatten the wire (*see* Working with Wire in Chapter 3) and join the ends of the wire together to create a circle.

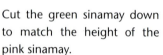

Cut the green sinamay down to match the height of the pink sinamay.

Measure the edge of the hat and cut a piece of wire to this measurement plus 4cm for crossover.

Cut a length of pink thread and run it through some beeswax to strengthen it.

Attach the wire to the hat at four points – use the 3, 6, 9 and 12 o'clock positions as before.

Sew the wire onto the hat using wire stitch (*see* Stitches in Chapter 3).

Cut a piece of petersham ribbon the length of the edge of the hat plus 4cm. Fold the petersham in half and curve with an iron (*see* Disc Headpiece with Flower in Chapter 5).

Sew the petersham onto the hat using a slip stitch, and then moisten the edge of the petersham to shrink it (*see* Covering the Wire with Petersham in Chapter 3).

Once the petersham is dry, it sits flat around the brim.

The lime-green petersham provides an effective contrast on the pink brim.

Add the trims. This hat uses a pink feather mount with wire running through it, which enables the feathers to be curved to the shape of the brim. Use tie tacks to secure. Add the green hackle feathers individually and glue in place.

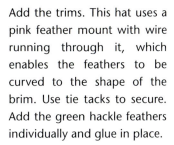

Ensure the feathers are balanced and the placement of the green feathers is adding to the overall effect of the finished hat. Keep the green feathers in one area to empha-size the contrast with the pink feathers and to pick up the green of the petersham trim. Add a sinamay flower with rolled edges to each petal. Secure the flower in place and add a headband or comb to secure the hat to the head.

Buckram Base Covered with Woven Fabric

Oval blocked buckram base covered with pink woven fabric and trimmed with a bow in the same fabric.

Buckram is a very versatile material to use within millinery; the sizing or glue that infuses the fabric dries to keep any shape into which the buckram has been blocked. Use two layers of buckram when blocking to give the final hat the strength it will need.

Buckram is very pliable when wet and, despite being quite messy to work with, takes on different shapes well. It is quite usual for the buckram to need to be blocked more than once to get the final folds out of the shape and to create finer details. Whilst this can be time-consuming, it is worth taking this time to perfect the shape.

Using a buckram base enables almost any flat fabric to be made into a hat. The base provides the perfect foundation over which to stretch a top fabric, turning any fabric into a millinery fabric. This creates potential for great variety to the finish of your hats.

For this hat, the buckram is blocked over a small oval dome block and the finished hat perches at the front of the head, attached with an elastic that secures under the hair. The fabric was chosen so that the woven lines and the texture of the fabric accentuate the shape of the hat.

You will need:

domed block	cotton-covered millinery wire
buckram	iron-on interfacing
top fabric	cling film
hat elastic with metal ends	heat-proof gloves
thread that matches the colour of the top fabric	scrap of fabric
needle	iron
pins	buckram, fabric and paper scissors
beeswax	pattern paper
	hem turner

Use a small wooden domed block – a small fascinator-size block for a small perching hat. Cover the block with cling film.

Ensure that the piece of buckram is big enough to cover the block.

Once the buckram is blocked and dry (*see* Chapter 3), remove from the block. Measure the circumference of the block and cut a piece of wire to this measurement plus 4cm extra for crossover.

Flatten the wire (*see* Working with Wire in Chapter 3) and join the ends together to create a circle. Coat your thread with beeswax before sewing the wire onto the edge of the buckram using wire stitch.

Cut a piece of iron-on interfacing big enough to cover the hat.

Protect your hands with heat-proof gloves and hold a balled-up piece of fabric inside the hat. Using a small iron on a low setting, carefully iron the interfacing onto the hat. Start in the middle of the hat and work towards the edges.

Ensure the interfacing is attached over the edge of the hat where the buckram curves under. Cut off any excess once the interfacing has cooled.

Cut a piece of top fabric on the bias that is large enough to easily cover the hat shape.

Pin the fabric in place and sew it with thread that matches the top fabric. Coat the thread with beeswax and keep the stitches on the right side of the hat very small so they do not show.

For the bow trim, cut out a rectangle of top fabric. It is easiest to cut out a template in paper first to check the size against the hat.

Fold the rectangle in half and sew the open edges on a sewing machine, leaving a small gap for turning. Trim the corners off at a 45-degree angle, being careful not to cut the stitching.

Turn the rectangle through the gap and use a hem turner to push out the corners.

Make a second, slightly smaller, rectangle in the same way as the first and press both to flatten the seams. Sew up the gaps in the rectangles by hand using slip stitch.

Place the smaller rectangle on the larger rectangle and wrap the bias binding around to create a bow. Sew the binding at the back and trim off any excess. Finally, sew the bow onto the hat and remove any

Create a small piece of bias binding for wrapping around the rectangles (*see* Three-Section Constructed Buckram Headpiece in Chapter 6).

remaining pins. Try the hat on and place a pin on either side of the hat where the natural side points are. Turn the hat over and push the metal ends of the elastic through the base; make a small hole in the base first if necessary.

Felt Pork Pie-Style Hat

Felt is the easiest and most forgiving material to block with, so it is a great material for the novice milliner to use and gives really beautiful results. Felt hoods are available in different sizes and the weight of the felt can vary. Heavier felts need to be steamed for longer than lighter felts to make them pliable for blocking. The finish of the felt also has a bearing on how easy it is to block. Fur felts are often easier to block, but are much more expensive to buy than wool felts and perhaps should be used once confidence with blocking has been achieved.

For this hat, a round pork pie-style all-in-one block is used. This block has a presser that is purchased with the block to place on top of the blocked felt. The presser pushes the felt into the indentation and helps to create the detailing as the felt dries. This avoids having pinholes in the surface of the finished hat. The feather trim and vintage-style button in a bright colour contrasts with the chocolate base and add height and movement to the hat.

Pork pie-style blocked felt hat in chocolate wool felt with trims in contrast orange.

You will need:

pork pie-style crown block
brown felt
lining fabric
orange petersham ribbon
five orange feather trims
orange button
thread that matches the colour of the felt
needle
pins
cotton-covered millinery wire
cling film
fabric scissors
steam iron

1

Use a pork pie-style crown block for this hat. Cover with new cling film before blocking.

Block the felt over the block. Carefully steam the felt and push into the indentations. Roll a length of fabric and pin through this and the felt into the block and leave to dry.

2

Pin the felt to the block, stretching it around the shape of the block. Pin into the block at the point where the curved edge meets the underside of the block.

Once the felt is dry, take out the pins and remove the felt from the block. Cut the excess felt back to the pin line.

Measure the circumference of the hat and cut a piece of wire to this measurement plus 4cm extra for crossover. Flatten the wire (*see* Working with Wire in Chapter 3) and then join the ends together to create a circle. Sew into the felt. Keep the stitches very small on the right side of the hat.

Attach the feathers to the hat together and cover the stitches with a tie of matching orange petersham ribbon.

Spread the feathers out over the hat and adjust the heights.

Bunch together five feathers – the ones used here have been cut to give an arrow effect.

Add a button to the tie for a focal point and to hide the stitches that attach the feathers to the hat. Line the hat with a disc of fabric sewn into the edge felt and slipstitch petersham ribbon around the head fitting.

Straw Peaked All-In-One Hat

Straw can be more difficult to block with, but once the basic technique is mastered, the effects are worth it and show off the natural texture of the material.

The difference to blocking straw as opposed to felt is that straw is woven, whereas felt has no weave. Straw has the vertical and horizontal lines of the pieces of straw that make up the fabric of the material and when blocking, this weave must be taken into account. If there is a certain section of the straw that needs to be blocked, it cannot be flattened to the block by pulling down and out as with felt. The line of the weave must be followed to the edge of the straw. This means that to flatten a section of the straw, it may be necessary to actually pull the edge of the straw 10cm or more to the side of this section. This takes some getting used to but is very effective. Straw can be blocked or ironed to stretch and shape it, as in the brim of this hat.

A vintage-style round pointed block is used

A blocked hat made using a straw parasisal hood in orange with a hand-shaped brim and a petersham trim.

to form the initial shape of this hat. The brim is then manipulated by hand and the hat is trimmed with petersham ribbon.

1

Use a crown block with sloped sides and a pointed crown. Cover the block with cling film.

You will need:

block with sloped sides and pointed crown
straw hood with textured surface
cling film water spray
plastic bag
steam iron
thread that matches the colour of the straw
 and petersham
needles
pins
cotton tape
snips and buckram scissors
craft knife
tape measure
cotton-covered millinery wire
petersham ribbon in a contrasting colour

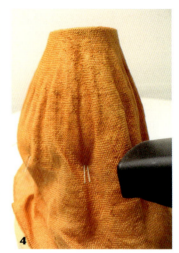

A straw hood with a textured surface in a bright orange is used for this hat.

Spray the hood with a mist of water all over and then fold into four. Place into a plastic bag, tie up and leave for ten minutes.

Steam the hood and pull over the block shape. Steam each section and then secure the hood with pins at the 3, 6, 9 and 12 o'clock positions.

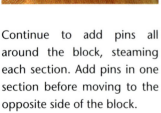

Continue to add pins all around the block, steaming each section. Add pins in one section before moving to the opposite side of the block.

Smooth out as many of the creases as possible. It may be necessary to move pins and re-steam sections to do this.

Once the pins are in all the way around, wrap cotton tape around the top of the block, as it is difficult to tighten up this area by blocking alone due to the shape. The cotton tape can be pulled tight and pinned in place.

Remove the cotton tape once the straw is completely dry. It may need to be left overnight.

Once the straw is dry, remove the pins and use a craft knife to make a cut in the straw. Use this to insert scissors and cut the excess straw away from the back of the block. This extra piece can be reused as a trim or a brim.

Leave the straw longer at the front as this will form the peak of the hat.

Continue to shape the straw until the desired design is achieved.

Use an iron on a medium temperature setting to iron the inside of the peak. This will stretch and smooth the straw.

Allow the straw to cool once the shaping is finished.

Measure the circumference of the hat including the brim and cut a length of wire to this measurement plus 4cm for crossover. Flatten the wire (see Working with Wire in Chapter 3), join the ends together to create a circle and then shape it to follow the lines of the hat.

Measure around the hat and cut the same length of petersham ribbon.

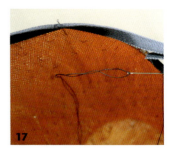

Fold the petersham in half and press with an iron. Curve the petersham with the iron (see Disc Headpiece with Flower in Chapter 5) and pin to the edge of the hat.

Sew the wire onto the hat by first attaching it at the 3, 6, 9 and 12 o'clock points. Using wire stitch, sew the wire onto the edge of the hat all the way around.

Sew the petersham onto the edge of the hat with small slip stitches.

Dampen the petersham with a wet cloth to shrink it and make it sit flat. Be careful not to wet the hat too much or the straw will soften.

Leave the hat aside to dry completely.

Position a piece of petersham over the hat as a trim following the line of the brim. This shows the curve of the straw in a simple but decorative way. Ensure the petersham is level on both sides and pin into place.

Sew the final piece of petersham in place. Use a running stitch and sew through the petersham and the straw to secure.

OCCASION HATS

Interest in millinery and the wearing of hats is increasing. There are now more outlets where hats are being sold than there have been for several decades. Hats can be found in specialist millinery boutiques, hats are available in bridal shops and hats are also sold in department stores.

Special occasions are still the times when we wear hats and headpieces to show ourselves off to our best advantage, to add glamour and to make that special occasion truly special. This is the area where all the skills and techniques shown throughout this book are brought together. The materials are finer and the finishing must be perfect. Trims can be extravagant and outrageous without being overdone.

Bridal headwear showing delicate lace and flower motifs.

Bridal Headwear

Some brides know that they want to wear a tiara and a veil, which look beautiful. However, there are other options for their special day.

Bridal headwear can be subtle and delicate; then again, if the right materials are used, the styling can be flamboyant whilst the overall effect is still gentle. This chapter shows different kinds of bridal headpieces, all of which have the potential to finish off a bridal look to perfection.

LEFT: **A collection of occasion wear hats ready to be worn to a variety of special occasions.**

Silk and Lace Teardrop Headpiece with Veiling

You will need:

head-shaped block

buckram

silk fabric

Chantilly lace

veiling

brooch

needle

thread

pins

cotton-covered millinery wire

headband or comb

transfer adhesive

Teardrop shaped headpiece covered in silk and Chantilly lace.

The base of this headpiece is made from two layers of blocked buckram (*see* Buckram Base Covered with Woven Fabric in Chapter 7). The teardrop shape is then marked on the curved blocked surface. Cut out a second teardrop-shaped piece of buckram and trim to a slightly smaller size. This will be the lining of the head-piece.

Once the headpiece shape is wired (*see* Wiring the Edge in Chapter 3), cover the base with a layer of silk. Here the silk has been pleated to give a starburst detail to the rounder part of the headpiece. Use transfer adhesive to keep the silk in place and wrap the edges around the underside of the base. Cover the lining piece of buckram in the same way.

3

Overlay the silk with a layer of Chantilly lace and pin carefully in place. Pay attention to where the pattern of the lace sits on the headpiece. Then slip stitch the lace to the edges of the silk on the underside of the headpiece. Remove any pins.

4

Place the headpiece onto the veiling and check the placement of the headpiece on the head.

5

Use a head-shaped block to shape the veiling (*see* Joined Discs Headpiece in Chapter 5).

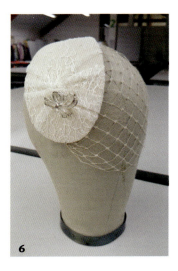

6

Place a brooch, hat pin or flower in the centre of the starburst. Often a bride will have an heirloom brooch she wants to wear, or will want to bring in the colour theme of the wedding by adding a matching flower here.

7

Secure the veiling to the headpiece with small slip stitches through the joins in the veiling. Once the veil is attached, the lining piece can be slip stitched in place. Try to ensure these stitches are invisible. The lining piece will give strength to the headpiece and hide the construction.

8

The finished headpiece sits to the side of the head with the veil just covering the face over one side. The veil can be made shorter or longer as desired. Attach the headpiece to either a metal headband or a comb depending on preference.

Lace Motif Headpiece

You will need:

buckram
dupion silk fabric
1 lace motif
chiffon or velvet ribbon
needle and thread
steam iron
buckram scissors and fabric scissors
transfer adhesive

A headpiece created from a lace motif mounted on a buckram base with a ribbon to secure it to the head.

Cut out a piece of buckram in the shape of the body of the lace motif. Cover this with dupion silk (pewter grey used here).

Cut out a lace shape from a piece of lace fabric.

Iron the silk onto the transfer adhesive. Then cut out the silk with a 1cm seam allowance around the buckram shape. Cut the seam allowance into tabs and fold these around to the wrong side.

Use transfer adhesive to attach the silk to the buckram shape. Iron the transfer adhesive onto the buckram using the backing paper to protect the iron.

Place the lace shape over the silk-covered side of the buckram. Stitch the lace to the buckram base with a matching thread. Hide the stitches in the pattern of the lace and keep the stitches very small so they do not show.

Draw around the buckram shape on another piece of silk to cover the underside of the buckram shape. Add a 1cm seam allowance to the shape and fold this seam allowance under at the edge. Use transfer adhesive to iron the silk onto the buckram and slip stitch the two layers of silk together.

Cut a piece of chiffon or velvet ribbon long enough to run across the width of the buckram base, wrap around the head and tie in a bow under the hair.

Pin the ribbon in place on the underside of the buckram base and try on for placement. Be careful of the pins. Once the ribbon is in the right place, sew it to the buckram base and remove pins.

Fan-shaped Headpiece

You will need:

crinoline
lace motifs
thread in a colour to match or invisible thread
polystyrene head
needle
pins
snips and fabric scissors
metal comb

A fan-shaped head piece made from crinoline and decorated with lace motifs.

Fold a piece of crinoline in half to create a folded edge. This becomes the short edge at the front of the headpiece.

Sew a line of large stitches along the long side from the folded edge to the back of the head-piece. Gather these stitches to create the fan shape.

Make a second fan shape in the same way to give the headpiece height and body.

Layer the two fans together to give the headpiece extra body.

Choose a piece of lace fabric with embroidered patterns on a tulle base.

Cut out the embroidered motifs with small sharp snips. Cut the joins of the tulle without snipping the embroidery.

Pin the crinoline fans onto a polystyrene head and place the embroidered motifs onto the crinoline.

Pin the embroidered motifs in place and remove from the polystyrene head.

Separate the layers of crinoline and pin motifs to the other layer too. Sew the motifs to the crinoline with either same colour thread or invisible thread if the motif is quite transparent.

Attach the two layers of crinoline together by stitching through with invisible thread. Cut out a round piece of embroidery from the pattern and apply to the crinoline as a central feature.

The edges of the crinoline that are at the back of the headpiece can be finished by folding the raw edge under and sewing down this seam with invisible thread using small stitches. Finally, sew a comb to the underside of the fans.

Mother of the Bride Hats

Every mother of the bride wants to look and feel fantastic on such a special day. This could be one of the only occasions when she feels it's right to wear a hat or headpiece.

Mother of the bride hats tend to fall into two categories: a small headpiece with plenty of feathers, height and movement (as described in Chapter 4) and a 'proper hat' with a brim and an impact all of its own.

These hats are great fun to make as they allow for the use of luxurious fabrics and bigger styles. It is essential, however, that these hats are comfortable to wear and lightweight. This means choosing the material and the style carefully.

White sinamay blocked hat with black sinamay trim and feather bunch.

Blocked Sinamay Hat in Black and White

You will need:

a crown block and a brim block
white and black sinamay
white petersham ribbon
goose biot feathers in black and white
   thread to match the sinamay

needle
pins
thimble
snips, buckram and paper scissors
iron

Block the crown of the hat in two layers of white sinamay over a rounded crown block (*see* Chapters 3 and 7).

Block the brim of the hat in two layers of white sinamay over a brim block that has a downward slope.

Once blocked and trimmed, the two pieces can be sewn together and the head ribbon sewn in place inside the head fitting. Use a white petersham for this.

Cut a bias strip of black sinamay long enough to sit around the crown.

Sew the band at the centre back and press the seam open.

Make a thin piece of bias binding (*see* Three-Section Constructed Buckram Head-piece in Chapter 6) in black sinamay to wrap around the base of the band. This gives the band definition and also covers the join between the two hat pieces.

Add a bundle of mixed black and white goose biot feathers. Curl these feathers by running the feather along the blade of a pair of paper scissors.

White Fur Felt One-Piece Hat

You will need:

crown block
white fur felt
mink fur felt for trims
white petersham ribbon
fabric leaves
needle
matching thread
pins
cotton-covered millinery wire
cling film

Fur felt hand-manipulated blocked crown and brim. This hat is decorated with flowers handmade in fur felt.

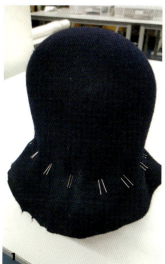

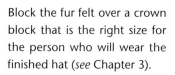

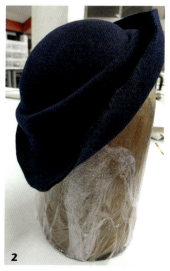

Block the fur felt over a crown block that is the right size for the person who will wear the finished hat (*see* Chapter 3).

Once the felt is dry, begin to manipulate the shape of the crown and create folds in the sides. This hat is to sit on the side of the head, so the crown is asymmetric.

Continue to fold the sides of the felt until the crown is created and the sideband is a ridge that sits around the crown. The rest of the felt becomes the brim.

Cut a piece of wire that fits around the edge of the brim. Flatten the wire (*see* Working with Wire in Chapter 3) and bend to fit the shape of the brim.

Sew the wire to the edge of the brim using wire stitch (*see* Chapter 3).

Pin the petersham ribbon in place and then slip stitch it to the felt. Ensure you keep the workspace and your hands clean if working with white fabric.

Ensure the stitches are neat and the wire is securely attached to the brim.

8

9

10

It is important to ensure that trims look right with the design, so use some felt scraps to try out some design ideas.

Run a damp cloth around the edge of the attached petersham. It will shrink slightly as it dries and it will sit flatter to the hat edge.

The edge will now be much flatter and the stitches will not show if they are very tiny.

11

Often there are colours or accessories that need to be matched when making a hat for an occasion. This hat has mink-coloured flowers and leaves.

This hat design can have trims on the crown and under the brim too.

12

Buckram Wide-Brimmed Hat

You will need:

crown block

buckram

top fabric and more to make bias binding

fabric to make flowers

a button for the centre

silk lining fabric

Paris net

matching thread and contrasting thread

needle

pins

thimble

cling film

buckram scissors and fabric scissors

cotton-covered millinery wire

Buckram wide-brimmed hat covered with pale green silk and a flower trim.

For the crown, block the lining fabric on the bias and then layers of Paris net and buckram over this.

The top fabric layer of silk is the last layer to be blocked.

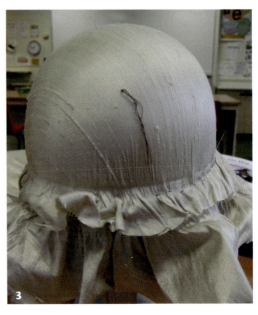

Mark the centre back with a tacking thread in a contrasting colour.

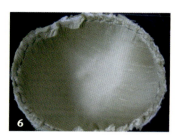

Once all the layers are dry, remove from the block.

Cut the excess layers from the base of the crown.

Trim the crown down to the level required.

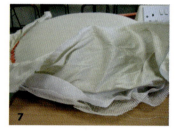

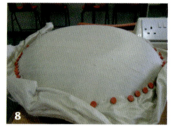

Block the brim over a brim block using the same layers of fabric as for the crown.

Stretch the foundation materials over the brim block and finish with the top fabric. Ensure the surface is as smooth as possible.

Sew a head wire to the brim (*see* Working with Wire in Chapter 3) and then remove from the block.

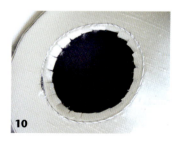

Measure 2cm inside the head wire and cut this hole out. Cut the 2cm seam allowance into tabs for attaching to the crown. Attach the wire to the edge of the brim.

Measure the outside edge of the brim and make a strip of bias binding (*see* Three-Section Constructed Buckram Head-piece in Chapter 6) in the top fabric to this measurement. Pin onto the brim and sew to the lower edge to the brim.

Fold the binding down and around the edge of the brim and slip stitch to the underside.

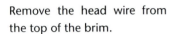

Remove the head wire from the top of the brim.

Fold the tabs inside the brim.

Measure the inside of the brim head fitting and make a length of bias binding the same length. Sew the binding into a loop using a diagonal join.

Wire the base of the crown, attaching the wire using wire stitch.

Insert the crown into the brim and line up the base of the crown with the head fitting of the brim. Cover this join with bias binding to neaten.

Finally, ensure the angle of the brim is correct. The hat should stay on the head as the crown fits over the head, but add a comb if necessary. Add trims to the finished hat. The instructions for the flowers used here can be found in Chapter 2.

SUPPLIERS

Millinery Suppliers

Petershams Millinery
3 Creekside, London SE8 4SA
Tel: 020 8469 0352
www.petershams.com

Baxter Hart and Abraham Ltd
141 New Bedford Road, Luton, Beds LU3 1LF
Tel: 01582 721381
www.baxterhart.org

Parkin Fabrics
Prince of Wales Business Park, Vulcan Street,
Oldham OL1 4ER
Tel: 0161 627 4455
www.parkinfabrics.co.uk

Atelier Millinery
Inside the Revival Retro Boutique
30 Windmill Street, London W1T 2JL
Tel: 0207 734 3848
www.ateliermillinery.com

MacCulloch & Wallis
25–26 Poland Street, London W1F 8QN
Tel: 020 7629 0311
www.macculloch-wallis.co.uk

Fabric and Haberdashery Suppliers

Whaleys (Bradford) Ltd
Harris Court, Great Horton, Bradford,
West Yorkshire BD7 4EQ
Tel: 01274 576718
www.whaleys-bradford.ltd.uk

A One Fabrics
50 Goldhawk Road, London W12 8DH
Tel: 020 8740 7349

A to Z Fabrics
53 Goldhawk Road, London W12 8QP
Tel: 020 8222 6566

Goldbrick Fabrics
20 Goldhawk Road, London W12 8DH
Tel: 020 8743 2744

Classic Textiles
44 Goldhawk Road, London W12 8DH
Tel: 020 8743 3516
www.classic-textiles.com

The Berwick Street Cloth Shop
14 Berwick Street, London W1F 0PP
Tel: 020 7287 2881
www.theberwickstreetclothshop.com

Misan
52 Berwick Street, London W1F 8SL
Tel: 020 7734 5441
www.misan.co.uk

Broadwick Silks
9–11 Broadwick Street, London W1F 0DB
Tel: 020 7734 3320
www.broadwicksilks.com

Truro Fabrics
Calenick Street, Truro TR1 2SF
Tel: 01872 222130
www.trurofabrics.com

John Lewis
300 Oxford Street, London W1C 1DX
Tel. 020 7629 7711
www.johnlewis.com

Dunelm
Various branches across the UK
www.dunelm.com

Hat Block Makers

Hat Blocks Direct
Unit 6A, Dial Estates, Dial Lane, Stourbridge, West
Midlands DY8 4YP
Tel: 07896 065402 or 01384 262259
www.hatblocksdirect.co.uk

Guy Morse Brown
Units 20–22, Jockey Lane Workshops, Bromham,
Wiltshire SN15 2EZ
Tel: 01380 859756
www.hatblocks.co.uk

INDEX